RYAN GIGGS
FIFTY DEFINING FIXTURES

Tony Matthews

Front and back cover photo courtesy of Malcolm Armstrong.

First published 2015

Amberley Publishing
The Hill, Stroud
Gloucestershire, GL5 4EP

www.amberley-books.com

British Library Cataloguing in Publication Data.
A catalogue record for this book is available from the British Library.

ISBN 978 1 4456 4678 7 (print)
ISBN 978 1 4456 4679 4 (ebook)

Typesetting and Origination by Amberley Publishing.
Printed in the UK.

Dedication

This book is, of course, dedicated to Ryan Giggs OBE, who else!

Acknowledgements

I would like to thank Richard Davidson, Brian Philipps and the man who helped with my *Manchester United Encyclopedia* back in 2002, John Robinson, for supplying and confirming certain match details. I would also like to thank Vanessa Le, Alan Murphy and Amberley Publishing for their assistance.

Contents

Personal Information

Name: Ryan Joseph Giggs, OBE

Born: Ryan Joseph Wilson

Birth place: St David's Hospital, Canton, Cardiff, South Wales

Birth date: 29 November 1973

Education: Grosvenor Road Primary and Moorside High Schools, Salford

Football career: Deans FC (as a schoolboy), Salford Boys, Salford Juniors, Manchester City (School of Excellence), Manchester United (trialist, aged fourteen, signed November 1987, turned professional November 1990); named interim player-manager at Old Trafford, April 2014; retired as a player, May 2014; continued thereafter as coach/assistant-manager to Louis van Gaal; also co-owner of Salford City FC; also played for England schoolboys, Wales (youth, U21 and senior levels) and Team GB (Great Britain, Olympic Games).

Introduction

Ryan Giggs was born to Danny Wilson, a rugby union player for Cardiff RFC, and Lynne Giggs (now Lynne Johnson). Of mixed race, his paternal grandfather comes from Sierra Leone and, in fact, has spoken of the racism he faced as a child. As a young boy Ryan grew up in Ely, a suburb of western Cardiff, with his younger brother, Rhodri. He spent a great deal of his time with his mother's parents, playing football and rugby whenever he could out on the streets close to their house in Pentrebane.

In 1980, when Ryan was just six years old, his father switched rugby codes from Union to League and signed for the Swinton club, which meant that the whole Giggs family had to move north to Swinton, a town in the City of Salford, Greater Manchester. The switch from South Wales to Lancashire proved to be a traumatic one as Ryan was very close to his grandparents in Cardiff and, in fact, he would often return there with his family at weekends and on school holidays. After moving to Salford, Ryan played football for his school team and his talent was quickly spotted by Manchester City's scout Dennis Schofield, who recommended that he should join Deans FC to gain some competitive experience.

Unfortunately Ryan, aged eleven at the time, didn't have the greatest of starts with Deans, being on the wrong end of a 9-1 defeat in his first game! However, he did show signs of quality and was given a trial by Salford Juniors. This time he was a star performer, scoring six goals for the 'B' team in an emphatic 8-1 win. Impressed with his progress, scout Schofield arranged a trial for Ryan at the Maine Road club and within a matter of days he was recruited to Manchester City's School of Excellence while continuing to play for Salford Boys, whom he helped reach the final of the Granada Schools Cup competition, which took place at Anfield.

Ryan, who chose to wear a red Manchester United t-shirt every time he turned up for training, captained the Salford team to victory over Blackburn Rovers in the final, being voted 'Man of the Match'. He collected the silver trophy from former Liverpool legend, and then the club's chief scout, Ron Yeats. The following season, Ryan played for Salford Juniors U16 side in the National final against St Helens at Old Trafford. Although he was on the losing side this time round, he had fulfilled an ambition by appearing on the same pitch as some of his heroes, including George Best and Bobby Charlton. He realised at this point that he wanted to get back there as soon as possible!

Besides playing football as a schoolboy, Ryan also enjoyed a game of Rugby League and represented his school and starred for the Salford District XV. In fact, he was all set to have a trial with the Great Britain team but circumstances prevented him from turning out – because he had just signed for Manchester United! However, while he was playing for Deans FC, Ryan was continually being watched by a local newsagent, an Old Trafford steward by the name of Harold Wood. Wood, in due course, spoke personally to Manchester United manager Alex Ferguson, who was intrigued with what he had heard and sent a scout to watch Ryan in action. The scout was very impressed with what he saw and, with Fergie's acknowledgement, offered Ryan a trial over the 1986 Christmas period. Ryan took part in a pre-arranged match between Salford Boys and United U15s side at The Cliff and with the United manager in attendance, looking on from his office window, he produced a fine display and scored a hat-trick in a 4-3 win. Giggs had produced the goods; Fergie was delighted with what he had seen and on 29 November 1987 he turned up at the Giggs' household (Ryan's fourteenth birthday). Old Trafford scout Joe Brown was also present as Fergie offered Ryan a two-year associate schoolboy contract. United, in fact, agreed to waive YTS forms and chose to give Ryan the opportunity to sign a professional contract in three years' time, when he was seventeen.

Under the name of Wilson, Ryan captained England schoolboys in 1988/89, helping them beat Belgium 3-1 in front of 40,000 fans at Wembley. He also starred in a 5-0 battering of Wales and in solid victories over both Germany and Holland who, of course, were bitter foes of the English at senior level!

Overall, Ryan played in nine U15 schoolboy internationals for England, seven of which resulted in victories. At the age of sixteen, Ryan elected to change his surname to that of his mother (Giggs) when his mother remarried, two years after separating from his father.

Ryan impressed everyone, manager, coaches, scouts, fellow players, young and old, over the next three years, and was offered his first professional contract on 29 November 1990, to celebrate his seventeenth birthday. He accepted the contract without much ado and became a full-time professional at Old Trafford two days later, on 1 December 1990. At the time, United were the FA Cup holders, having beaten Everton at Wembley, this being Fergie's first major prize following his arrival from Aberdeen in November 1986.

After two under-par seasons in the First Division which saw them finish in mid-table, United at last started to threaten the dominance of Liverpool and Arsenal, although they only managed a sixth-place finish in 1987. Fergie's quest for a successful left-winger had not been an easy one. Indeed, following the departure of Jesper Olsen two years earlier, and seeing Ralph Milne have more bad days than good ones, he signed the Southampton winger Danny Wallace in September 1989, but he too failed to shine at Old Trafford.

By the time Ryan had turned professional, Wallace was contesting the wing position with nineteen-year-old Lee Sharpe.

Ryan, after some very good Second XI displays, was called up for his League debut against Everton at Old Trafford on 2 March 1991, coming on as a substitute for the injured full-back Denis Irwin in a 2-0 defeat. That didn't matter to Ryan really ... he knew deep down he was on his way to the top! In his first full start, against rivals City in the Manchester derby two months later, he thought he had bagged his first ever goal, the winner in a hard-earned 1-0 victory – although it later appeared in the books as a Colin Hendry own goal!

Ryan was not included in United's sixteen-man squad that defeated Barcelona in the UEFA Cup Winners' Cup final eleven days later, Lee Sharpe being handed the left wing position, with Wallace on the subs' bench. Ryan didn't have too long to wait ... becoming a first-team regular early in the 1991/92 season while also remaining a vital member of United's youth team, which he captained to victory in the 1992 FA Youth Cup final.

Ryan had, of course, broken into United's first team at the age of seventeen, and his presence effectively led to many more of Fergie's fledglings taking the step up towards the senior XI. As the youngest member of the United first-team squad at the time, Ryan looked up to the older players such as Bryan Robson for advice. 'Robbo' recommended that Ryan sign up with agent Harry Swales who was, at the time, looking after the interests of Kevin Keegan.

That season – 1991/92 – Ryan starred in the team that finished as runners-up to Leeds United in the final year of the old First Division before the advent of the Premier League. Fergie's team had led the table for much of the season before a run of disappointing results in April saw them overtaken by the West Yorkshire side. That campaign was not all despair for United, or Ryan, who collected his first piece of silverware on 12 April 1992 when Nottingham Forest were defeated in the League Cup final at Wembley, Ryan having a hand in the game's only goal, scored by Brian McClair. At the end of the season, Ryan was voted PFA Young Player of the Year – the award which had been won by his club teammate Lee Sharpe twelve months earlier.

By the start of the first ever Premier League season in 1992/93, Ryan had ousted Sharpe to become United's first-choice left-winger. And he was quickly recognised as being one of the country's two best emerging young wingers, along with Liverpool's Steve McManaman. Both players were noted at the time for being throwbacks to the Stanley Matthews era of the 1950s winger. Ryan duly helped United to their first top-division title win for twenty-six years, making forty-one appearances and scoring nine goals.

His emergence, and the arrival of Frenchman Eric Cantona, heralded the dominance of Manchester United in the Premier League. Boss man Fergie was very protective of Ryan, refusing to allow him to be interviewed until he had turned twenty. He eventually granted his first interview to Des Lynam on the BBC's *Match of the Day* programme in 1993/94.

United won the double that season, Ryan being one of the key players, along with Cantona, Paul Ince and Mark Hughes. Ryan also played for United in the Football League Cup final but this time finished up a loser, as Aston Villa won 3-1.

Off the pitch, newspapers claimed that Ryan had 'single-handedly revolutionised football's image' when he appeared as a teenager 'with pace to burn, a bramble patch of black hair bouncing around his puppy pop star face, and a dazzling, gluey relationship between his impossibly fleet left foot and a football'.

As a result of all this publicity, he was afforded many opportunities not normally offered to footballers at such a young age, such as hosting his own television show, *Ryan Giggs' Soccer Skills*, which was first aired in 1994. He also had a book based on the series published.

At this juncture, Ryan became part of the Premier League's attempt to market itself globally. He was featured on countless football and lad (boy) magazine covers, thus becoming a household name and fuelling the era where footballers started to become celebrity idols, on a par with pop stars. By the mid to late 1990s and despite his aversion to attention, Ryan also became a teenage pin-up and was once described as the 'Premiership's First Poster Boy' and the 'boy wonder.'

By now hailed as the first football star to capture the public imagination since the days of former United great George Best, the irony was that 'Bestie' along with Bobby Charlton, used to describe Ryan as their favourite young player. Indeed, they turned up at the club's Cliff training ground just to watch him. Best once quipped, 'One day they might even say that I was another Ryan Giggs'.

At the end of the 1993/94 campaign, Ryan helped United clinch their second Premier League title in a row, and at the same time became the first player in history to win two consecutive PFA Young Player of the Year awards, a feat later equaled by Robbie Fowler and his future United teammate Wayne Rooney.

Ryan also began to prove himself as a scorer of great goals, many of them being short-listed for various 'Goal of the Season' awards. Some of his finest which quickly come to mind are those he netted against Queens Park Rangers in 1993, Tottenham Hotspur in 1994, Everton in 1995, Coventry City in 1996 and his magnificent solo effort in extra time of the 1999 FA Cup semi-final replay against Arsenal at Villa Park. That evening, he picked the ball up in his own half of the field, after Patrick Vieira, had lost possession. Setting off on a mazy dribble which took him past and round the entire Gunners' back line, including Tony Adams, Lee Dixon and Martin Keown, he then launched a booming left-footed shot which fizzed into the net, high past a startled David Seaman.

Ryan then celebrated by famously whipping off his shirt as he ran down the pitch back to the dugout. The marvelous strike also has the distinction of being the last ever goal scored in an FA Cup semi-final replay as, from the following season, the competition's semi-finals comprised a single game, with extra time and a penalty shoot-out if required deciding who went forth to the final.

In the 1994/95 season, due to injury, Ryan made only twenty-nine Premier League appearances, scoring just one goal. However, late in the season, he rediscovered his form and his fitness, but his return to action came far too late, as United ended the campaign without a single trophy to their name.

Failure to beat West Ham United on the final day of the season resulted in the Reds being pipped to the Premier League title by Blackburn Rovers, and a week later Ryan came on as a substitute in United's 1-0 FA Cup final defeat at the hands of Everton.

On a more positive side, in the 1994/95 season, Ryan featured on the scoresheet twice in United's opening Champions League game against IFK Gothenburg, which resulted in a 4-2 win, although the Reds ultimately failed to make it through to the quarter-finals. He also netted in the FA Cup fourth round victory over Wrexham, meaning that he had managed to score in all major competitions that season.

In 1995/96 Ryan, back to full fitness and in good form, played a vital part in United's unique second double, his goal against Everton at Goodison Park in early September being short-listed for the 'Goal of the Season' award. In the end, a strike by Manchester City's Georgi Kinkladze was voted the best.

In November of that season, Ryan bagged two goals in a 4-1 Premier League win against Southampton, which kept the pressure on Newcastle United, who actually went ten points clear at the top of the table forty-eight hours before Christmas. But as the Geordies' form dipped, so United's picked up and they eventually overhauled the team from the north-east in mid-March.

Ryan played for United in the 1996 FA Cup final victory over Liverpool, Eric Cantona scoring the vital goal, and at this juncture the Welshman had been joined in the team by several youngsters including the Neville brothers, Gary and Phil, Nicky Butt, David Beckham and Paul Scholes. Beckham, in fact, replaced Andrei Kanchelskis on the right wing while Butt succeeded Paul Ince to complete a new-look United midfield along with Ryan and hard man Roy Keane.

The following season, Ryan was given the opportunity to show off his talent in Europe. Having been a vital member of United's third Premier League title-winning team in four seasons, he helped the Reds reach the semi-finals of the Champions League, the first United side in twenty-eight years to go this far in the prestigious competition.

However, hopes of European glory ended at the hands (or rather feet) of Borussia Dortmund, who edged through to the final, winning both legs 1-0 for a 2-0 aggregate victory.

At the end of this season, Juventus' Alessandro Del Piero informed the Italian media that Ryan was one of his two favourite footballers, revealing, 'This is embarrassing to say, but I have cried twice in my life watching a football player; the first one was Roberto Baggio and the second was Ryan Giggs.'

In 1997/98, United were once again pipped to the Premier League title, this time by Arsenal. This was down to a dismal run of form in March and early April, and as a result they ended the campaign without a trophy for only the second time since 1989.

The following season, Ryan missed quite a few games with niggling injuries, but when he did play his form was excellent and he starred in both of United's cup finals after his superb extra-time goal in the FA Cup semi-final replay against Arsenal earned United a 2-1 win and his 90th minute equaliser in the home leg of the UEFA Champions League semi-final against Juventus set up a meeting with Bayern Munich in the Champions League final.

In the latter, United trailed 1-0 with time fast running out. Indeed the clock showed 90 minutes when they won a corner on the left. Ryan swung the ball over but it was short of the danger zone and came back out to him. This time he drove it low into the box where Teddy Sheringham swooped to notch the equaliser. Seconds later, Ole Gunnar Solskjaer poked in the winner. What a finish, what a night. United had won the treble! And they soon made it four trophies in a year after beating Palmeiras to claim the Intercontinental Cup, Ryan being named 'Man of the Match' after another inspirational performance.

Ryan continued to excel in the four years that followed United's treble-winning season and the team went on to win the Premier League title three times in four seasons, as well as reaching the Champions League quarter-finals on three occasions and the semi-finals once. As a result of all this success, in April 2001 Ryan was offered a new five-year contract by Alex Ferguson, and he had no worries whatsoever about signing it!

Ryan duly celebrated his ten-year anniversary at Old Trafford with a testimonial match against Celtic at the start of the 2001/02 season. In a game of very few tackles, and with Eric Cantona making a cameo appearance, the Scots won 4-3.

Unfortunately, 2001/02 turned out to be one of the most disappointing seasons United had endured since Ryan made his senior debut, as a horrible run of results in early winter ultimately cost them the Premier League title. They were also surprisingly eliminated from the Champions League on the away goal rule in the semi-finals by German underdogs Bayer Leverkusen.

On a brighter note, in May 2002, Ryan became United's longest serving player when full-back Denis Irwin left Old Trafford for Wolves. At the time, he was a pivotal part of the team, despite being only twenty-eight years old.

On 23 August 2002, Ryan reached a personal milestone when he netted his 100th career goal in United's draw with Chelsea at Stamford Bridge.

But after that, Ryan amazingly lost his form! He defended himself by insisting that he was not finished and that this hiccup on the field would soon be rectified. He missed an open goal during a 2-0 defeat against Arsenal in the FA Cup in mid-February – describing it at the time as the worst miss of his career – and it prompted chants from the Arsenal fans of 'Give it to Giggsy'.

However, a week later, he bounced back and produced one of his most memorable displays, helping United to a resounding 3-0 victory over Juventus.

An 8th-minute substitute for Diego Forlan, he netted twice, including a superb strike that would later be heralded as one of his greatest goals he ever scored and one of the finest Champions League moments of his career.

Around this time in 2003, Ryan was reportedly close to joining the Italian club Internazionale Milan in a swap deal involving Adriano, but he immediately quashed the rumours by saying, 'I'm staying put; I'm happy at United'.

Ryan appeared in his fourth FA Cup triumph on 22 May 2004, making him one of only two players (the other being Roy Keane) to have won the trophy four times while playing for Manchester United. He went on to collect a total of three runners-up medals as well, in 1995, 2005 and 2007.

His participation in the Premier League victory over Liverpool in September 2004 made him only the third player to appear in 600 senior games for United, the others being Sir Bobby Charlton and defender Bill Foulkes.

A year later Ryan was inducted into the English Football Hall of Fame in recognition of his contribution to the English game and, of course, to Manchester United.

In 2005, Ryan's form had improved considerably and he was no longer suffering with those tedious hamstring injuries which had plagued his career, attributing it all to taking up yoga! As his career progressed, Ryan abandoned his position on the left wing, manager Fergie giving him a more central role in midfield.

He duly signed a two-year extension to his contract when the club's Chief Executive David Gill relented on his normal policy of not giving players over the age of thirty a contract longer than one year. Ryan was a special player, however, and he benefited greatly from being largely injury-free and he went on to have a very sound 2006/07 season.

He scored his first goal of the campaign (the winner) in a 2-1 Premier League encounter against Watford in late August 2006; struck the decider (an 8th-minute header) in United's next game, a 1-0 home victory over Tottenham Hotspur and netted with another smart header from Cristiano Ronaldo's cross and swung over a free kick for Nemanja Vidic to score in United's final Champions League group game against Benfica in December.

And things got better. In February 2007, he netted the first of his last three goals of his season in a 4-0 away win against Tottenham, which sent United six points clear of Chelsea at the summit of the Premier League. He then scored the winner against Lille in the Champions League when his quickly taken free kick caused the French team's players to walk off the pitch in protest, and he notched an equaliser against Fulham in a game which United went on to win thanks to a late Ronaldo winner which extended their lead over Chelsea to nine points. Talking about his free kick against Lille, Ryan said, 'I was amazed by the situation, as no rule had been broken.'

On 6 May 2007, Chelsea could only manage a 1-1 draw with Arsenal in the London derby. This left them seven points behind Manchester United with only two games remaining, and therefore the Reds were declared Premier League champions for the ninth time. As a result, Ryan set a new record by featuring in all of those nine triumphs and therefore beat the previous record of eight winner's medals gained by the Liverpool duo of Alan Hansen and Phil Neal.

In the 2007 FA Cup final against Chelsea, Ryan had an extra-time goal ruled out by referee Steve Bennett who deemed him to have fouled goalkeeper Petr Čech in forcing the ball across the line. Chelsea went on to win the trophy.

A few months later, Ryan (and United) were back at Wembley for the annual FA Community Shield, and once again their opponents were Chelsea. This time it was an entirely different story as Ryan scored an equaliser in the first half (1-1) and then netted from the spot in the penalty shoot-out, which United won 4-3 after goalkeeper Edwin van der Sar had saved all of Chelsea's first three penalties. This spot-kick 'goal' was, in fact, Ryan's first as a professional at Wembley Stadium.

In 2007/8, United's boss Alex Ferguson adopted a new system whereby he utilised Ryan with newcomers Nani and Anderson, rarely playing all three together.

Ryan scored his 100th League goal for United against Derby County in December 2007, helping United to a 4-1 win. And more landmarks soon followed: on 20 February 2008 he made his 100th appearance for the club in the Champions League (*v.* Lyon) and on 11 May 2008, in a 2-0 away win over Wigan Athletic, he came on as a substitute for Park Ji-Sung to equal Sir Bobby Charlton's record of 758 senior appearances for United, and he scored to celebrate the occasion. Now a true United legend, Ryan fired in the second goal in the match against Lyon and his strike at Wigan sealed his, and United's, tenth Premier League title.

Ten days later, on 21 May 2008, he broke Charlton's appearance record for United when he came on as an 87th-minute substitute for Paul Scholes in the Champions League final against Chelsea. United won the game 6-5 on penalties (following a 1-1 draw after extra time) and it was the cool-headed Ryan who effectively converted what proved to be the winning spot kick in sudden death.

At the start of the 2008/09 season, Sir Alex Ferguson chose Ryan in central midfield, behind the strikers, instead of his favoured wing position. Fergie said in an interview,

He [Giggs] is a very valuable player; he will be thirty-five this November and can still be United's key player. At twenty-five, Ryan would shatter defenders with his run down the flank, but at thirty-five, he will play deeper.

At this time, Ryan was talking seriously about taking his coaching badges and Fergie hinted that he would like his star man to assist on his coaching staff after retirement. Following speculation earlier in the year, in February 2009 Ryan signed a one-year extension to his contract, which was set to expire in four months' time.

After a successful season, Ryan was short-listed, along with four other Manchester United team-mates, for the PFA Player of the Year. On 26 April 2009, he was presented with the award, despite having started just twelve games during the 2008/09 season at the time of him receiving the trophy. This was the first time in his career that Ryan had received this top award and it was a fitting tribute to his long-term contribution to the game.

Ryan went on to make his 800th first-class appearance for Manchester United on 29 April 2009, starring in the 1-0 Champions League semi-final first leg win over Arsenal. He celebrated again soon afterwards when the Gunners were licked 3-1 in the return leg at The Emirates.

On 16 May 2009, United won the Premier League again, after a 0-0 draw with Arsenal, and it was, of course, both United's and Ryan's eleventh Premier League titles. Some record.

After so many years and hundreds of games Ryan, at long last, scored his first Manchester United hat-trick in a pre-season friendly against Hangzhou Greentown in July 2009, claiming the feat as a second-half substitute.

Barely two months later, on 12 September 2009, Ryan made his 700th start for United and he quickly followed up with his 150th goal for the club, becoming only the ninth player to achieve this milestone, when he found the net against Wolfsburg in his first Champions League game of the season.

On the eve of his thirty-sixth birthday, 28 November 2009, Ryan scored his 100th Premier League goal – all for United – in a comfortable 4-1 victory over Portsmouth at Fratton Park. At the same time he became only the seventeenth player to reach the milestone in the competition (1992–2009).

Twenty-four hours after turning thirty-six, it was reported publicly that Ryan would be offered an additional one-year contract by United which would run until the end of the 2010/11 season. It would also see him pass the twentieth anniversary of his first game and first goal for the Old Trafford club. On the very same day, Ryan was nominated for the 2009 BBC Sports Personality of the Year, which he subsequently won ahead of F1 racing driver Jenson Button and world heptathlon champion Jessica Ennis.

'This is a shock as you can tell by the speech I've prepared,' joked a totally surprised Ryan as he collected his award, 'I grew up watching this programme. To see the people that have won it and to be here is unbelievable.'

Ryan was the first footballer to lift the prestigious trophy since England midfielder and his former Old Trafford colleague David Beckham in 2001. Only five soccer stars have actually won the award, the other three being Michael Owen in 1998 (who also played for United during his career), Paul Gascoigne in 1990 and Bobby Moore in 1966.

A fortnight before Christmas 2009, Ryan surpassed fellow Welshman Gary Speed's record of 535 appearances by an outfield player in the Premier League. This came a week after he had signed that one-year contract extension with United, keeping him at the club until June 2011 and on New Year's Eve he was officially named as Manchester United's Player of the Decade, some honour considering the other stars who had been associated with the club.

On 24 April 2010 Ryan, somewhat surprisingly perhaps, scored the first ever 'League' penalties of his career. In fact, he netted two spot kicks in a 3-1 home Premier League win over Tottenham Hotspur and 75,268 fans were there to see him double up! Four months later, in August 2010, Ryan maintained his record of scoring in every Premier League season since its inception in 1992, netting United's third goal in a convincing 3-0 home victory over Newcastle United in their opening fixture of the new campaign. And as he had previously found the net in the final two seasons of the old Football League First Division, he had now scored in twenty-one successive top-flight campaigns. Terrific stuff.

On 17 January 2011, Ryan reached another milestone ... his 600th League appearance in a goalless draw with Tottenham at White Hart Lane. Then, the very next month, and still looking pretty active and injury-free, he duly signed yet another one-year extension to his contract with United, tying him to the club until the summer of 2012. It was record-breaking time again on 6 March 2011, when Ryan surpassed Sir Bobby Charlton's record of 607 'League' appearances for the club when he took the field in a 3-1 defeat at Liverpool.

Then, some seven weeks later, in late April, when playing against FC Schalke 04 in the Champions League semi-final first leg, Ryan netted the first goal from Wayne Rooney's pass to become the oldest goalscorer in Champions League history at that time. Ryan then played in the Champions League final, which United lost 3-1 to Barcelona.

Ryan made his first start of the 2011/12 season in the away Champions League encounter with Benfica, scoring United's equalising goal in a 1-1 draw at the Estádio da Luz. This strike saw him break his own record of being the oldest goal scorer in Champions League history. He also became the first player ever to score in sixteen different Champions League campaigns, taking over the mantle previously held by the former Real Madrid forward Raúl, who was tied with Ryan on fifteen seasons. The Spaniard, however, still holds the competition record for scoring in fourteen consecutive seasons.

On 19 November 2011, Ryan played in a League game in his home country of Wales for the first time ever, for United against Swansea City at the Liberty Stadium. United won the game 1-0. Ryan maintained his record of scoring in each top-flight season since 1990 by grabbing United's third goal against Fulham at Craven Cottage in a 5-0 romp shortly before Christmas 2011 – this being his first of the season at League level.

And then, as a belated Christmas (or New Year's) present, he signed yet another one-year contract extension with United in February 2012, shortly before making his 900th club appearance in United's 2-1 away win over Norwich City. And he marked the occasion by scoring the winning goal in the 19th minute from Ashley Young's splendid cross. After the match at Carrow Road, Alex Ferguson told BBC Sport he believed that a player playing in 900 games for one club 'won't be done again'.

By March 2011, Ryan had lined up with more than 140 different players for Manchester United at first-team level. And that is also a record!

Moving on, eighteen months later, on 19 October 2012, Ryan, whose thirty-ninth birthday was only a month away, told *Daily Telegraph* that he would like to move into management when he retires as a player. He also said that he was still undecided on whether he would still be playing after the current football season ended.

As per usual, Ryan began another term as a member of United's first team squad, but he had a long wait before scoring his first Premier League goal of 2012/13, obliging in a 2-0 home win over Everton in the February, extending his goal-scoring sequence to twenty-three consecutive seasons in the highest division, including all twenty-one Premier League seasons.

Ryan was at it again on 1 March 2013 when he put pen to paper by signing a new one-year contract with United, which would keep him at Old Trafford until June 2014. And during the summer of 2013 he was appointed as player/coach by new manager David Moyes, who had taken over from Sir Alex.

Ryan was appointed player/coach at Old Trafford on 4 July 2013, as part of the coaching staff under Moyes. And when Moyes was sacked on 22 April 2014, after fewer than ten months in the job, Ryan took over as the club's interim player/manager, compiling a record of two wins, a draw and a defeat in the final four games of the 2013/14 season.

After his final match in charge, a 1-1 draw with Sunderland, Ryan admitted to breaking down in tears, in part due to the pressure of managing United, and said that he had struggled to sleep during the period. He was, however, praised for giving debuts to youngsters James Wilson and Tom Lawrence in a 3-1 victory over Hull City, a game in which he brought himself on as a substitute for Lawrence.

When Louis van Gaal was announced as Moyes' permanent replacement on 19 May 2014, Ryan became the Dutchman's assistant manager and coach.

Harking back to 2 October 2013 … after coming off the bench against Shakhtar Donetsk, Ryan became the all-time leading appearance-maker in the Champions League, overtaking Raúl, an achievement he described as something special.

The following month, Ryan celebrated his fortieth birthday, leading to media outlets and football figures praising him for reaching the milestone. However, as expected, Ryan officially announced his retirement as a player on 19 May 2014 and the letter saying so was openly posted to all Manchester United fans on the club website.

Upon his retirement, Ryan received many plaudits for the achievements he earned throughout his career and his longevity … and it isn't over yet!

International career

Born in Cardiff, to Welsh parents, Ryan represented Wales in full internationals having captained England schoolboys as a teenager, but, contrary to popular belief, he was never eligible for the full England team. Eligibility at the schoolboy level depends solely upon the location of the school, and in Ryan's case it was Moorside High School in Salford.

In October 2009, new rules were introduced for the Home Nations' Associations that would have enabled Ryan to play for England had he not already represented Wales in an official competition, but Ryan has always maintained that he would have chosen to play for Wales anyway, saying in 2002,

I'd rather go through my career without qualifying for a major championship than play for a country where I wasn't born or which my parents didn't have anything to do with.

In his one year as an England schoolboy player, Ryan appeared in nine games, all as captain, winning seven and losing twice. The wins included a 4–0 victory over his Welsh peers, many of whom he would eventually play alongside, and against, as he rose through the ranks. In May 1991, Ryan made his debut for the Welsh U21 team in a 2-1 win over Poland in Warsaw. This would be his only appearance at this level, as he gained a call-up to the senior team later in the year.

Ryan made his full international debut away to Germany in October 1991, coming on as an 84th-minute substitute for Eric Young at the age of seventeen years, 321 days, making him the youngest player to win a full cap for Wales. He held the record until June 1998, when another Ryan – Green, of Wolves – played against Malta at the age of seventeen years, 226 days.

Wales were well in contention to qualify for Euro 1992 before that game, but suffered a 4-1 defeat; this allowed Germany, who won their remaining games against Belgium and Luxembourg, to pip them at the post.

Ryan's first senior goal for Wales came on 31 March 1993, in a 3-0 World Cup qualifying win over Belgium in Cardiff. Ian Rush scored his record 24th goal for Wales in this game.

After his international debut in 1991, Ryan missed eighteen consecutive non-competitive matches before finally making his first friendly appearance against Finland in March 2000, by which time he had already gained twenty-five caps.

The reason for his continued absence from friendly fixtures was largely a protective measure against unnecessary injuries. In his autobiography, Ryan states,

> At that time, whenever I played two games in one week I always seemed to pick up an injury, so (Alex Ferguson) and I sat down and looked at it game by game. If the international was a friendly, the feeling was that I didn't have to play.

Wales lost a 2006 World Cup qualifier 2-0 to England at Old Trafford in October 2004. Ryan played in that match, lining up against present and former Manchester United teammates David Beckham, Gary Neville, and Wayne Rooney. And during another qualifier, versus Azerbaijan a year later, he notched a rare double in a 2-0 win, but sadly Wales failed to reach the play-offs.

In September 2006, Ryan lined up for his country in a 2-0 friendly defeat by Brazil at White Hart Lane. After the game, visiting coach Dunga congratulated Ryan on an excellent performance, admitting that he would not look out of place playing for the five-time world champions alongside stars such as Kaká and Ronaldinho.

At a pre-arranged press conference at The Vale of Glamorgan Hotel on 30 May 2007, Ryan told reporters that he will shut the door on a sixteen-year career with Wales in three days' time – after his sixty-fourth and final game for the Red Dragons in a Euro 2008 qualifier against the Czech Republic at Cardiff. He led the team in a 0-0 draw.

Ryan said that he wanted to concentrate wholly on his United career – this being the main reason for stepping down. Five months after retiring, Ryan was one of three players named in the final nomination by the FAW for the Wales Player of the Year award, which was ultimately won by Craig Bellamy.

In an interview with the *Western Mail* on 26 March 2010, Ryan hinted that he might be tempted to come out of international retirement for his country's Euro 2012 qualifying campaign, in order to cover for the injured Aaron Ramsey. He later clarified his position to BBC Radio Manchester, saying that he would only return to international duty in an emergency. Nothing materialised.

On 28 June 2012, Ryan was confirmed as one of the three over-age players selected in Team GB's squad to compete at the 2012 Summer Olympics, the other two being Bellamy and the Manchester City defender Micah Richards. Ryan was given the captaincy as Great Britain fielded a soccer team for the first time in forty years.

Ryan scored with a header against the United Arab Emirates in a 3-1 win in a Group game to become the oldest goal-scorer in the football competition at the Summer Olympics. He was thirty-eight years and 243 days old, beating an eighty-eight-year-old record that had been held by Egypt's Hussein Hegazi.

Discipline

Ryan was never sent off in twenty-four seasons of first-class football with Manchester United, but he was dismissed playing for Wales against Norway in a World Cup qualifier on 5 September 2001 after committing a second yellow card offence in the 86th minute of a 3-2 defeat in Oslo.

In November 2003, Ryan was found guilty of improper conduct by the FA following some unprecedented behaviour during the 'Battle of Old Trafford' game with Arsenal – being one of two United and six Arsenal players charged over the on-field incident. He received a £7,500 fine but avoided suspension.

In the same week, Ryan received a two-match suspension from international football for deliberately elbowing Russian player Vadim Evseev in the face during the first leg of a Euro 2004 play-off encounter. The incident was missed by referee Lucílio Batista, but Ryan was later charged after the official panel had studied the match video.

Career Statistics with Manchester United

	F/L P/L		FA Cup		League Cup		Europe		Others		Total	
	Apps	Goals	Apps	Goals	Apps	Goals	Apps	Goals	Apps	Goals	Apps	Goals
1990–91	2	1	0	0	0	0	0	0	0	0	2	1
1991–92	38	4	7	0	8	3	1	0	1	0	51	7
1992–93	41	9	2	2	2	0	1	0	0	0	46	11
1993–94	38	13	7	1	8	3	4	0	1	0	58	17
1994–95	29	1	7	1	0	0	3	2	1	0	40	4
1995–96	33	11	7	1	2	0	2	0	0	0	44	12
1996–97	26	3	3	0	0	0	7	2	1	0	37	5
1997–98	29	8	2	0	0	0	5	1	1	0	37	9

(Continued...)

	F/L P/L		FA Cup		League Cup		Europe		Others		Total	
	Apps	Goals	Apps	Goals	Apps	Goals	Apps	Goals	Apps	Goals	Apps	Goals
1998–99	24	3	6	2	1	0	9	5	1	0	41	10
1999-00	30	6	0	0	0	0	11	1	3	0	44	7
2000–01	31	5	2	0	0	0	11	2	1	0	45	7
2001–02	25	7	1	0	0	0	13	2	1	0	40	9
2002–03	36	8	3	2	5	0	15	4	0	0	59	14
2003–04	33	7	5	0	0	0	8	1	1	0	47	8
2004–05	32	5	4	0	1	1	6	2	1	0	44	8
2005–06	27	3	2	1	3	0	5	1	0	0	37	5
2006–07	30	4	6	0	0	0	8	2	0	0	44	6
2007–08	31	3	2	0	0	0	9	0	1	1	43	4
2008–09	28	2	2	0	4	1	11	1	2	0	47	4
2009–10	25	5	1	0	2	1	3	1	1	0	32	7
2010–11	25	2	3	1	1	0	8	1	1	0	38	4
2011–12	25	2	2	0	1	1	5	1	0	0	33	4
2012–13	22	2	4	1	1	2	5	0	0	0	32	5
2013–14	12	0	0	0	2	0	7	0	1	0	22	0
Totals	672	114	74	12	41	12	157	29	19	1	963	168

Record with Wales (Full International Level)

Year	Apps	Goals
1991	2	0
1992	3	0
1993	6	2
1994	1	1
1995	3	0
1996	3	1
1997	3	1
1998	1	0
1999	3	1
2000	4	1
2001	4	0
2002	5	0
2003	7	1
2004	3	0
2005	6	3
2006	5	0
2007	4	1
Total	64	12

Team GB Olympic Football Team

Year	Apps	Goals
2012	4	1
Total	4	1

Managerial record (22 April–11 May 2014)

P	W	D	L	Win%
4	2	1	1	50.00

Club Honours - Manchester United

- Premier League (13): 1992/93, 1993/94, 1995/96, 1996/97, 1998/99, 1999/2000, 2000/01, 2002/03, 2006/07, 2007/08, 2008/09, 2010/11, 2012/13
- FA Cup (4): 1993/94, 1995/96, 1998/99, 2003/04
- League Cup (3): 1991/92, 2005/06, 2008/09
- FA Community Shield (9): 1993, 1994, 1996, 1997, 2003, 2007, 2008, 2010, 2013
- Champions League (2): 1998/99, 2007/08
- UEFA Super Cup (1): 1991
- Intercontinental Cup (1): 1999
- FIFA Club World Cup (1): 2008

Individual awards

- PFA Young Player of the Year (2): 1991/92, 1992/93
- PFA Team of the Year (6): 1992/93, 1997/98, 2000/01, 2001/02, 2006/07, 2008/09
- PFA Team of the Century (1): 1997/2007
- PFA Players' Player of the Year (1): 2008/09
- FWA Tribute Award: 2007
- Bravo Award (1): 1993
- BBC Sports Personality of the Year (1): 2009
- BBC Wales Sports Personality of the Year (2): 1996, 2009
- GQ Sportsman of the Year (1): 2010
- Sir Matt Busby Player of the Year (1): 1997/98
- Jimmy Murphy Young Player of the Year (2): 1990/91, 1991/92
- Premier League: 10 Seasons Awards (1992/93 to 2001/02): Overall Team of the Decade
- Premier League: 20 Seasons Awards (1992/93 to 2011/12): most Premier League

appearances in that time (598)
- UEFA Champions League, 10 Seasons Dream Team (1992-2002): 2002
- Wales Player of the Year Award (2): 1996, 2006
- Premier League Player of the Month (3): September 1993, August 2006, February 2007
- Goal of the Season prize (1): 1998/99
- English Football Hall of Fame Inductee: 2005
- Golden Foot award: 2011

Orders and Special Awards

- OBE for services to football: 2007
- Honorary Master of Arts Degree from Salford University for contributions to football and charity work in developing countries: 2008
- Freedom of the City of Salford: 7 January 2010 – being the twenty-second person to receive the Freedom of the City of Salford.

Records as a Player

- Won a record thirteen top-division English League/Premier League titles – the only Manchester United player to receive a winner's medals from all thirteen Premier League title wins.
- Most Premier League appearances for a player, with 632.
- Only player to have played in twenty-two successive Premier League seasons.
- Only player to have scored in twenty-one successive Premier League seasons.
- Only player to have scored in seventeen different Champions League tournaments (includes eleven consecutive tournaments, 1996/97 to 2006/07; only Raúl has a better record with fourteen)
- Most goals by a British player in the Champions League/European Cup proper history, and fourteenth overall (not including preliminary rounds).
- Most UEFA Champions League appearances.
- Most appearances by a Manchester United player.
- Most starts by a Manchester United player (794 games).
- First player to score 100 Premier League goals for Manchester United.
- Second midfielder to score a century of Premier League goals for a single club (the first was Matt Le Tissier, Southampton).
- One of four Manchester United players to win two Champions League medals (Paul Scholes, Gary Neville and Wes Brown are the others).
- Oldest player, aged thirty-seven years, 289 days, to score in the Champions League (*v.* Benfica on 14 September 2011).
- One of two Manchester United players to win at least ten top-division medals (the

other is Paul Scholes).

- Oldest player, aged thirty-eight years, 243 days, to score in the football competition at the Summer Olympic Games (*v.* United Arab Emirates on 29 July 2012).
- Made more appearances in the Manchester derby than any other player.

Endorsements and Public Image

Ryan has been featured in adverts for Reebok, Sovil Titus, Citizen Watches, Givenchy, Fuji, Patek Phillipe, Quorn Burgers, ITV Digital and Celcom.

In 2008, the National Library of Wales paid approximately £10,000 for Peter Edwards' portrait of Ryan Giggs, to be hung at their headquarters in Aberystwyth.

Personal Life

Ryan married his long-time partner, Stacey Cooke, in a private ceremony on 7 September 2007. They have two children, both born in Salford, and live in Worsley, Greater Manchester, close to where Ryan grew up as a young lad.

Activism

In August 2006, Ryan became an Ambassador for UNICEF UK, in recognition for his work with Manchester United's 'United for UNICEF' partnership with the children's organisation.

Ryan visited UNICEF projects in Thailand and he told the BBC, 'As a footballer I can't imagine life without the use of one of my legs ... Sadly this is exactly what happens to thousands of children every year when they accidentally step on a landmine'.

Post-playing Career

In October 2010, Ryan confirmed he would probably finish his career at Old Trafford and that he could not see himself dropping down leagues and playing at a lower level.

He admitted that he wanted to go into coaching, describing the management of Manchester United or Wales as 'the two ultimate jobs', and stating that he was halfway through his UEFA 'A' coaching licence.

Ahead of his testimonial in 2011, Gary Neville revealed he would put the proceeds towards a supporters' club and hotel near Old Trafford. Despite objections from Manchester United, Neville's plans were approved in 2012.

In 2013, Ryan joined forces with his former playing colleague Neville to launch a company named GG Hospitality, with plans to build football-themed hotels and cafés around the United Kingdom, initially in Manchester and London. The first operation was a football-themed restaurant – Café Football – in Stratford, London, which officially opened in November 2013. Then came Hotel Football, previously under the guise of the supporters' club, which Neville announced in 2011. This was scheduled to open in late 2014.

Earlier in 2014, it was announced that Ryan, along with four other United legends – Gary Neville, Paul Scholes, Nicky Butt, and Phil Neville – had agreed to purchase Salford City football club, ahead of the 2014/15 season, with plans to get the club to the Football League. The five-man group announced it would take part in a special friendly, with Salford facing United's Class of '92 team. On 22 September of that year, the group agreed to sell a 50 per cent stake in the club to billionaire Peter Lim.

Fifty Defining Matches

How does one even consider choosing fifty matches out of the 1,031 Ryan played at senior level for club and country? With great difficulty, I can honestly say. Reporting on 100 would be hard going, but I had to select just fifty which I feel were defining fixtures in the playing career of one of Manchester United's greatest ever players, Ryan Giggs. There are wins, defeats, even draws, disappointments and celebrations … enjoy and reminisce.

1

Manchester United 0 Everton 2
League Division One
2 March 1991

After some impressive displays for United's Second XI as well as producing the goods on the training ground, Ryan Giggs was named in the first team squad by manager Alex Ferguson for the home League game against Everton in early March 1991.

Lying fifth in the table and without a win in their last three games, United had not been playing well, while their Merseyside opponents had lost three of their previous four games and were also out of form.

Manchester United (3-4-1-2): Sealey; Irwin (Giggs), Donaghy, Pallister, Martin (Beardsmore), Blackmore, Ince, Ferguson, Sharpe, McClair, Wallace.
Everton (4-4-2): Southall; Hinchcliffe, Keown, Ratcliffe, Watson, McDonald, Ebbrell, McCall, Nevin (Atteveld), Newell, Sharp (Cottee).
Attendance: 45,656

The opening exchanges, on a heavy-looking pitch, were fairly even with Paul Ince, Darren Ferguson and Clayton Blackmore battling for midfield supremacy with Stuart McCall, John Ebbrell and McDonald. In fact, there were precious few chances at either end during a tentative opening quarter, although both McClair (United) and Newell (Everton) tried their luck from distance while Danny Wallace came close for the Reds.

The breakthrough finally arrived in the 33rd minute. Pat Nevin drove forward into the United half and fed Graeme Sharp to feet. The striker quickly played the ball forward to Ebbrell who was barged into by Gary Pallister just outside the United penalty area.

Andy Hinchcliffe struck the resulting free-kick hard and low through the wall to goalkeeper Les Sealey's right. The United number one saved low down but Mike Newell, following up, had the simple task of slotting the loose ball into the net from close range.

2 minutes after falling behind, United lost full-back Denis Irwin who went off injured. As a result, Ferguson switched his team around and brought on the fresh-faced Ryan Giggs for his senior debut. He was just seventeen years, three months and four days old.

However, before Giggs could get into the game, even touch the ball with any authority, Everton scored again.

A throw in on United's right in the 39th minute led to Hinchliffe delivering a high cross to the far side of the 18-yard box. The ball was quickly switched back into the danger-zone, which Mal Donaghy headed out for a corner. This led to another flag-kick on the opposite side of the field. Taken by Nevin, Sharp challenged Sealey in the air and, when the ball dropped, Dave Watson pounced to fire home from 6 yards.

United huffed and puffed during the second half. McClair (twice) and Giggs went close but Neville Southall, in all fairness, was hardly troubled. At the other end of the field Sealey saved well from Newell, while Everton substitutes Atteveld and Tony Cottee both flashed efforts inches wide.

As for Giggs, he did well, and afterwards his marker, Kevin Ratcliffe, said, 'I know now why his manager put him on at such a tender age. He has talent and will be a star of the future, mark my words.'

NB: Prior to Giggs' tender-age debut, the previous youngest United players had been goalkeeper David Gaskell, aged sixteen years and nineteen days in 1956, wing-halves Jeff Whitefoot, sixteen years and 105 days in 1950 and the great Duncan Edwards, sixteen years and 185 days in 1953, plus two sixteen-year-olds, winger Willie Anderson in 1963 and striker Norman Whiteside in 1982, while inside-forward Arthur Rowley, aged fifteen years and 222 days, had guested for United during the Second World War.

2

Manchester United 1 Manchester City 0
League Division One
4 May 1991

Unbeaten in seven League games prior to this encounter with neighbours City, United were holding their own in the First Division. They were lying fifth in the table with four matches remaining, although they had no chance at all of catching the top two, Arsenal and Liverpool. They did, however, want to finish ahead of their Manchester rivals who, with just two fixtures remaining, were in fourth place on 59 points, against United's 55.

Manager Alex Ferguson made five changes from the team that had beaten Derby County in the previous game, bringing in Ryan Giggs for his first start in a red shirt in place of Danny Wallace and naming Gary Walsh in goal.

City, meanwhile, were in good form, having battered Aston Villa 5-1 in their last game when David White netted four times.

Manchester United (4-4-2): Walsh; Irwin, Bruce, Pallister, Phelan, Blackmore, Webb, Robson, Hughes, McClair, Giggs (Donaghy).
Manchester City (4-4-2): Margetson; Hill, Hendry, Redmond, Pointon, White, Brennan (Reid), Ward (Clarke), Harper, Heath, Quinn.
Attendance: 45,286

There was a great atmosphere inside the ground when referee Peter Tyldesley got the game started but unfortunately there was not much excitement at either end of the pitch during the first 20 minutes, with both goalkeepers having very little to do.

But then, perhaps out of the blue, United took the lead in the 22nd minute. Denis Irwin pumped a hopeful ball down the middle, Mark Hughes cleverly flicked it on to Brian McClair who delivered a low cross into the City danger zone.

Arriving late was Ryan Giggs who gleefully scored his first ever senior goal ... and if the truth is known, there was more than an element of doubt about it!

The Welshman, in fact, to this day, is not sure whether or not he got a touch on the ball before City defender Colin Hendry did. However, one only has to look at the record books and it clearly says that the goal bagged by the then-teenager settled this derby in United's favour.

After that set back, City battled hard and long in search of an equaliser. White and Adrian Heath both went close and Niall Quinn missed with a clear header, while at the other end of the field, Giggs, Hughes, Bryan Robson, who was outstanding, and Neil Webb put efforts far too near keeper Martyn Margetson in the City goal.

The second half was much better than the first. United shaded it, just, and Hughes hit the woodwork. Late on substitute Wayne Clarke did likewise for City after Webb thought he had netted United's second goal, moments after referee Tyldesley had blown up for a foul by White on Clayton Blackmore, much to the annoyance of the United supporters and of course Webb himself. With time running out Robson came mighty close to scoring himself.

Over forty free kicks were awarded but it was not a dirty match and in the end United just about deserved to take the points.

After the game, Giggs said,

I ran across the face of the goal towards the near post, and stuck my foot out. I don't think I touched the ball with my boot, but perhaps my shoe laces did! People thought it was a Colin Hendry own goal. They may be right, but everyone came running across and started celebrating with me. I was certainly happy to be credited with the goal, especially as it beat our arch rivals City. The day couldn't have gone any better.

Surprisingly, Giggs (who was seventeen and a half at the time) was not included in United's squad of sixteen for the clash with Barcelona in the UEFA Cup Winner's Cup final in Rotterdam eleven days later ... a game United won 2-1.

3

Manchester United 3 Cambridge United 0
League Cup 2nd Round, 1st Leg
25 September 1991

After seeing his team thump Luton Town 5-0 in their home First Division game four days earlier, United's boss Alex Ferguson put out his strongest line-up for the visit of Cambridge United to Old Trafford. And before kick-off he asked his players to 'go out and express themselves' against John Beck's side who were in decent form, having won five of their opening eight League fixtures and were lying fourth in Division Two.

In the Cambridge line-up was striker Dion Dublin, who would subsequently join the Reds for £1 million in August 1992.

Manchester United (4-4-2): Walsh; Irwin, Bruce, Pallister, Blackmore, Phelan, Webb (Giggs), Robson, Ince, McClair, Hughes.

Cambridge United (4-5-1): Vaughan; Fensome (Clayton), Kimble, Bailee, Chappell, O'Shea, Cheetham, Wilkins, Dublin (Claridge), Taylor, Philpott.

Attendance: 30,934

This was a game United were expected to win ... and they did, but it wasn't easy! Cambridge played well and, in fact, they had two or three chances to take the lead before Ryan Giggs, on as a substitute for the injured Neil Webb, scored the opening goal of the tie a minute before half-time ... his first in the League Cup competition. United's goalkeeper Gary Walsh was the busiest of the two custodians in the first half, making two fine saves, while at the other end of the field, Vaughan was in the right position at the right time to deny both Brian McClair and Bryan Robson.

3 minutes after the interval the visitors fell two behind when McClair netted from close range and although United dictated possession for long periods, Cambridge certainly gave as good as they got with both Dublin and Lee Philpott going close.

It was effectively game over in the 66th minute when centre-back Steve Bruce bagged United's third goal, but late on substitute Steve Claridge came within a whisker of grabbing a consolation goal for the underdogs.

McClair and Giggs had late chances to increase United's lead, but in the end it was the Reds, deservedly so, who took the honours and after drawing 1-1 in the second leg in front 9,248 fans at Cambridge's compact Abbey Stadium (McClair scoring after just 2 minutes), they entered the third round of the competition as 4-1 aggregate winners, as they slowly but surely made their way to the final.

N.B. Twenty-three and a half years later, in January 2015, United beat Cambridge by the same score (3-0) in a 4th round FA Cup replay in front of more than 75,000 fans at Old Trafford, after a 0-0 draw at The Abbey Stadium.

4

Wales 1 West Germany 4
European Championship Qualifier
16 October 1991

Having beaten the Germans 1-0 at Cardiff Arms Park four months earlier, courtesy of an Ian Rush goal, Wales knew that a draw in Nuremberg would see them qualify for the 1992 European Championships as group five winners. Defeat, however, would give the Germans the advantage. They had a game in hand – against Belgium in Brussels – while both countries still had to play, and were expected, to beat, the minnows from Luxembourg.

Manager Terry Yorath named Ryan Giggs in his thirteen-man squad for the first time, placing him on the subs' bench.

West Germany (4-4-2): Ilgner; Binz, Rueter, Kohler, Buchwald, Brehme, Matthäus, Möller, Doll (Effenberg), Völler, Riedle (Hassler).
Wales (5-2-3): Southall; Bodin, Ratcliffe, Melville, Young (Giggs), Bowen, McGuire (Speed), Horne, Hughes, Rush, Saunders.
Attendance: 45,773

After a tentative opening 10 minutes when neither side threatened, the Germans took control, pegging Wales back in their own half of the field. Launching attacks at will down their left wing, with Lothar Matthäus instrumental in most things, the hosts scored three times in the space of 10 minutes to stun the visitors!

After having six shots and headers at Neville Southall's goal, Eintracht Frankfurt star Andreas Möller opened the scoring 34 minutes in. He took a left-wing corner, got the ball back before cutting inside to beat Southall with a low drive.

With Wales totally on the back foot, AS Roma striker Rudi Völler headed in a second goal on 39 minutes … a gift, following a horrid looped back pass by Swindon Town full-back Paul Bodin. And seconds before half-time, Lazio's Karl-Heinz Riedle nodded in another left-wing cross as the hosts simply took over the show.

With Giggs watching from the touchline, the Welsh defence had simply capitulated as the Germans powered forward in numbers.

Wales, who were reduced to ten men in the 51st minute when Dean Saunders was red-carded, conceded a fourth goal to another Lazio player, Thomas Doll, on 73 minutes. He found space to net with a low right-footer drive from 10 yards after Andy Melville had blocked an effort from Möller.

Wales rarely created a chance but they did get on the scoresheet in the 85th minute when Ian Rush was fouled inside the penalty area, allowing Bodin to bang home the spot kick.

Soon afterwards Giggs came on for his senior international debut (replacing defender Eric Young). He was just seventeen years and 321 days old – making him the youngest player to win a full cap for Wales at that time.

Unfortunately he hardly touched the ball as Berti Vogts' enterprising German side strolled to a comfortable victory.

Wales won their final game 1-0 against Luxembourg but Germany won their last two, beating Belgium 1-0 and Luxembourg 4-0 to qualify as group winners with 10 points, one more than unlucky Wales.

5

Manchester United 2 Middlesbrough 1
(After extra time, United won 2-1 on aggregate)
League Cup Semi-Final, 2nd Leg
11 March 1992

The first leg of this League Cup semi-final ended 0-0 at The Riverside Stadium in front of 25,572 fans. It was a close contest with the home side coming close to winning and reaching their first ever major Cup final. For the return leg at Old Trafford, Middlesbrough brought with them 9,000 fans, boosting the evening attendance to almost 46,000.

Alex Ferguson had centre-back Steve Bruce available (he had missed the first leg) and was therefore able to field his strongest side, with Ryan Giggs playing wide on the left allowing Brian McClair to go through the centre, supported whenever possible by Bryan Robson and Lee Sharpe.

'Boro manager Lennie Lawrence named former United junior goalkeeper Stephen Pears in his line-up.

United had already knocked out Cambridge United, Portsmouth, Oldham Athletic and Leeds United while 'Boro had ousted Bournemouth, Barnsley, Manchester City (2-1 in round four) and Peterborough United. In fact, 'Boro were in good form. They were lying fourth in Division Two, having lost only one of their previous seven League games and eight all season. Strikers Bernie Slaven and Paul Wilkinson had been scoring well and there was no doubt that they would pose a threat to United's back four.

Manchester United (4-4-1-1): Schmeichel; Parker, Bruce, Pallister, Irwin, Webb, Ince, Robson, Sharpe (Robins), McClair, Giggs.
Middlesbrough (4-4-2): Pears; Fleming, Kernaghan, Mohan, Phillips, Mustoe (Proctor), Pollock, Hendrie, Ripley (Falconer), Wilkinson, Slaven.
Attendance: 45,875

There was a terrific atmosphere inside Old Trafford when referee John Martin got the game underway and it was 'Boro, kicking towards the Stretford Road End and wearing light blue shirts and navy shorts, who had the first effort at goal, John Hendrie firing fractionally too high above Peter Schmeichel's crossbar from Alan Kernaghan's free-kick.

Soon afterwards a Paul Wilkinson header flew a yard over as Bruce and Gary Pallister back-pedalled.

United replied immediately and Denis Irwin was only inches wide with a crisp low volley.

On a slippery pitch, tackles were going in ten a penny and both Bryan Robson and Jamie Pollock were ticked off by the referee.

Giggs, who was already causing a few problems, then eased past Curtis Fleming as United came again but his cross lacked direction. Stuart Ripley was stopped in his tracks by Neil Webb before Robson fired over the top.

Wilkinson, the lively Slaven and Ripley all had efforts at goal, likewise Robson, Giggs and Sharpe for United before the latter finally broke the deadlock in the 29th minute.

Some sat that the goal came against the run of play but who cared … United were in front and on their way to Wembley.

'Boro though refused to lie down. They pushed forward in numbers and twice in quick succession Schmeichel at to be at his best to prevent an equaliser before half-time.

Like at the start of the first session, 'Boro came out of the blocks quickest and in the 50th minute they drew level through Bernie Slaven who slid the ball home from close range.

As delighted away fans raced onto the pitch, it took a posse of stewards and police to contain them.

United were stunned and it was all hands to the pump for the next 10 minutes or so as 'Boro came again. Thankfully, Bruce was at his very best, putting in two superb tackles to deny Wilkinson and Ripley.

United regrouped and certainly shaded the last quarter of normal time, Pears pulling off two fine saves in the 'Boro goal.

In fact, there were incidents aplenty at both ends of the pitch as the game headed into extra time. And as the minutes ticked by, it was 'Boro who regained the initiative. Indeed they looked the more confident side, knowing that if they could hold out for a draw they would go through to the final on the away goal rule.

United had to raise their game … and they did just that! 'Boro were pushed back and in the 109th minute Old Trafford erupted when Ryan Giggs was in the right spot at the right time to steer the ball past Pears from Robson knock down after Irwin's teasing cross.

At last United started to play and McClair and Giggs could have increased the scoreline before referee Martin blew his whistle for the last time to confirm United's place in the League Cup final for the third time, having previously lost in 1983 and 1991.

6

Manchester United 1 Nottingham Forest 0
League Cup Final
12 April 1992

Following their 1991 defeat at the hands of Sheffield Wednesday, United wanted to put that disaster behind them against Brian Clough's efficient Nottingham Forest side.

Forest, in fact, had already lifted the trophy four times (the same number as Liverpool) while United were seeking their first victory in the competition's thirty-two-year history, having also lost to Liverpool in the 1983 final.

At the time of this Wembley showdown, United were sitting on top of the Premier League, and were in decent form, having lost only one of their previous seventeen competitive matches. Forest, meanwhile, were down in tenth position.

Both captains – Bryan Robson (United) and Stuart Pearce (Forest) missed the game through injury. Alex Ferguson elected to go for Mike Phelan in midfield with the Ukrainian winger Andrei Kanchelskis being preferred to Lee Sharpe.

Manchester United (4-4-2): Schmeichel; Parker, Irwin, Bruce, Phelan, Pallister, Kanchelskis (Sharpe), Ince, McClair, Hughes, Giggs.
Nottingham Forest (4-4-2): Marriott; Charles (Laws), Williams, Walker, Wassall, Keane, Crosby, Gemmill, Clough, Sheringham, Black.
Attendance: 76,810

United, skippered by Steve Bruce, wore light blue flecked shirts and blue shorts against Forest's traditional red and white as County Durham referee George Courtney got the final underway in bright sunshine.

Without going too deeply into what happened out on the pitch, suffice to say, it was not the greatest of games ever staged at Wembley.

The final was decided as early as the 14th minute when Brian McClair scored for United … his twenty-third goal of the season.

The Scottish international striker, who minutes earlier had seen a 'goal' ruled out following a foul by Mark Hughes on Darren Wassall, found enough space between Forest defenders to hit a low left footed shot to the right of goalkeeper Andy Marriott after a smart reverse pass from Giggs who, of course, was playing in his first major Cup final.

After this breakthrough, Hughes and Paul Ince, had decent efforts to extend United's slender lead while future United stars Teddy Sheringham and Roy Keane both came close to equalising for Forest, as did the manager's son, Nigel Clough.

There were far too many fouls, nothing malicious, just niggles, during a lacklustre first half and the theme continued after the break, although Clough was only inches away from beating Schmeichel to his left with a rasping free kick from the edge of the area.

United perhaps played the better football, but there was something missing! Giggs carved out a few openings late on as legs tired, but unfortunately his crossing let him down, while Kanchelskis also failed to deliver from the flanks. He was eventually substituted by Sharpe with a quarter of an hour remaining.

After the game a delighted McClair said, 'I'm sure if Stuart Pearce had been playing I wouldn't have had the same chance. But all credit to Giggsy ... his return pass to me was spot on.'

As winners, United became the first losing finalists in the competition – after their loss twelve months earlier – to return in the next season and lift the trophy. This game was also notable as Brian Clough's last major domestic Cup final as a football club manager.

At the same time, it was Ferguson's fourth piece of silverware as United's boss in two years, following successes in the 1990 FA Cup and 1991 Cup Winner's Cup finals and in the 1991 UEFA Super Cup.

7

Manchester United 3 Crystal Palace 2
(United won 6-3 on aggregate)
FA Youth Cup Final, 2nd Leg
15 May 1992

Having won the first leg 3-1 at Selhurst Park in front of just 7,825 fans, United were beaming in confidence as they took the field for the return clash at Old Trafford.

Ryan Giggs, who had missed the first leg, came into United's team in place of Robbie Savage, who dropped to the substitute's bench. Also lining up for United were future stars John O'Shea, David Beckham, Nicky Butt and Gary Neville, while the Palace team included striker George Ndah who would go on to score almost eighty goals in a little over 300 club appearances during his fourteen-year professional career.

On their way to the final, United had eliminated Sunderland, Walsall, Manchester City (3-1), Tranmere Rovers and Tottenham Hotspur (5-1 on aggregate), while Palace had knocked out Charlton Athletic, Chelsea (2-0), Crewe Alexandra, West Ham United (also 2-0) and Wimbledon (5-4 over two legs).

The scene was set for a cracking second encounter.

Manchester United (4-3-3): Pilkington; O'Kane, Switzer, Casper, Neville, Beckham, Butt, Davies (Gillespie), McKee, Giggs, Thornley (Savage).
Crystal Palace (4-4-2): Glass; Sparrow, Cutler, Holman, Edwards (Watts), McPherson, Hawthorne, Rollison (Daly), McCall, Ndah, Clark.
Attendance: 14,681

Ryan Giggs skippered United who were made to fight every inch of the way by a resolute, plucky and determined Palace side who gave absolutely everything they had.

Giggs, who of course was already a first-teamer at Old Trafford, had two early efforts at goal, as did Butt who netted twice in the first leg at Selhurst Park; Beckham scored the other.

Palace, though, were just as dangerous and it was they who took the lead when Andy McPherson rose to meet Scott Cutler's corner to power a header past United goalkeeper Kevin Pilkington.

United's nerves were eased, however, before half-time when Ben Thornley collected a smart pass from Simon Davies and cut inside his marker before confident slotting the ball past the advancing Jimmy Glass to make it 4-2 on aggregate.

Early in the second half, United went 2-1 up on the night when Davies rammed home a rebound after George Switzer's shot was saved. But gutsy Palace came again and Niall Thompson equalised by punishing defensive hesitancy with a fiercely struck drive from just outside the penalty area, netting with a shot which Pilkington had no chance whatsoever of saving!

United, however, still had something left in the tank and, following a swift passing movement involving Beckham, Butt and Giggs, the latter crossed perfectly from the left for Colin McKee to head home a third goal.

Late-on, substitute Savage and McKee came close to adding to United's score while, at the other end of the field, Ndah forced Pilkington into a sprawling save.

This was United's seventh victory in the annual FA Youth Cup final, having previously won the trophy in 1953, 1954, 1955, 1956, 1957 and 1964. And for Ryan Giggs, it was his second winner's medal in just five weeks. What a way to start your professional career.

And for the record, this United youth team became known as the 'Class of '92'.

8

Manchester United 5 Coventry City 0
Premier League
28 December 1992

Forty-eight hours before this game, United had drawn 3-3 away at Sheffield Wednesday while Coventry City were beating Midland rivals Aston Villa 3-0 at Highfield Road. In fact, United were unbeaten in six Premier League games and were sitting third in the table, whereas the Sky Blues hadn't lost in five and were lying in seventh position.

Both managers (Ferguson and Bobby Gould) were able to field their strongest sides, the latter naming his son, Jonathan, in goal as well as including former England and Arsenal player Kenny Sansom at left-back.

Manchester United (4-3-2-1): Schmeichel; Parker, Bruce (Phelan), Pallister, Irwin, Sharpe, Ince, Cantona, McClair, Giggs (Kanchelskis), Hughes.
Coventry City (4-4-2): Gould; Atherton, Borrows, Babb, Sansom, McGrath, Hurst, Rosario, Gallacher, Williams (Ndluvo), Quinn.
Attendance: 36,025

In front of the biggest Old Trafford crowd of the season (at that time) City had a couple of chances early on before United settled down with McClair and Hughes threatening.

The first goal came in the 6th minute, scored by Ryan Giggs with a superb left-footer after some smart work by Brian McClair and Eric Cantona. But although United were in command, City were always dangerous on the break, Micky Quinn testing Peter Schmeichel with a smart right-footer.

After holding out, with a certain amount of luck, City's defence conceded a second goal 5 minutes before half-time.

Mark Hughes, had already seen three efforts saved by keeper Gould and Cantona had been denied a headed goal by an offside flag. The former burst through and took McClair's pass in his stride before firing low past Gould's left hand to make it two-nil.

Although they held their own during the first 20 minutes of the second period, City fell further behind on 64 minutes when Frenchman Eric Cantona converted a penalty awarded for handball by Phil Babb, who had moved across into the left-back position.

After twice going close, Lee Sharpe burst onto the scene in the 78th minute to score United's fourth, driving the ball into the ground and over Gould following a deft downward header by Cantona. And after Giggs had been replaced by Andrei Kanchelskis, Hughes missed from close range before left-back Denis Irwin moved forward to bang in United's fifth goal 7 minutes from time, his right-footer being deflected into the net by the boot of unlucky defender Brian Borrows.

At this point City were spent and in the dying minutes United could and should have added to their goal-tally, but all credit to Gould who saved well from Hughes and Sharpe.

Referee Ron Groves had a good game. He was efficient and allowed play to run freely most of the time.

NB: Coventry had arrived at Old Trafford expecting to provide a stiff test for the resurgent Reds. However, United were in no mood to entertain the idea that Coventry might be a match for them and in the end they won comfortably. And the fact that five different players scored the goals clearly highlighted what a strong team United were and how many attacking options they had.

This victory sent United to the top of the table for the first time that season and paved the way for a tremendous second half to the campaign which saw them lose only twice on their way to claiming their first Premier League title under Alex Ferguson.

9

Wales 2 Belgium 0
World Cup Qualifier
31 March 1993

After spending virtually a year and a half as a named substitute for his country, being called into action just five times, Ryan Giggs finally made his full international debut in a vital World Cup qualifying game against Belgium in front of a highly emotional Welsh crowd inside Cardiff Arms Park Stadium. Wales simply had to win this game to keep in touch with the Group 5 leaders and manager Terry Yorath knew that his only option was to name an attacking line-up. He did just that and it paid off.

At the time Wales – who had recently attained their highest ever FIFA ranking – had already beaten the Faroe Islands 6-0 and Cyprus 1-0 but had lost heavily to Romania 5-1 in Bucharest and 2-0 against Belgium in Brussels. They couldn't afford to lose this encounter, knowing they still had to play all the big boys again before the qualification campaign ended in mid-November, with the USA beckoning!

Wales (4-3-3): Southall; Aizlewood, Young, Ratcliffe, Bodin, Horne, Speed (Phillips), Rush, Hughes, Saunders, Giggs (Bowen).
Belgium (5-4-1): Preud'homme; Grün, Staelens, Medved (Oliveira), Albert, Smidts, Boffin, Van der Elst, Scifo, Degryse, Czerniatynski (Severeyns).
Attendance: 27,002

The early exchanges were cautious, with both sets of defenders taking the easy way out by clearing their lines with huge kicks downfield or into touch. Wales looked the more nervous and both Gary Speed and Mark Hughes lost possession in crucial areas, while the Belgian Enzo Scifo had the first effort on goal.

After a couple of surges down either flank, the ground erupted in the 18th minute when Wales took the lead. Awarded a free kick on the edge of the penalty-area by referee Aron Schmidhuber, two players ran over the ball before Giggs moved forward behind them to smash an unstoppable left-foot shot past Michel Preud'homme. What a goal! It was quite brilliant and Wales were on the march.

Ian Rush went close again soon afterwards, as did Marc Degryse and Danny Boffin for the visitors, before the Cardiff crowd went into raptures again in the 39th minute as Wales scored a second goal.

Some precise and quick passing sent Dean Saunders clear down the left and from his high cross, delivered from off the by-line, Rush rose to head home from close range. With their fans jumping and dancing all around the ground, Wales were in control and it continued like that for the remainder of the first half and into the second period before Belgium started to threaten, albeit rather tamely!

But Neville Southall and his defenders were in no mood to concede and, as the minutes started to tick by, the crowd continued to roar their heroes on to a memorable victory.

Van der Elst came closest for Belgium while Saunders tested Preud'homme in the Belgium goal, and, with victory sewn up, manager Yorath brought on Mark Bowen and David Phillips late on to bolster up the back division and midfield.

This victory over Belgium was a great boost for Welsh football. And everyone knew they were mighty close to qualifying for the 1994 World Cup finals in the USA. But they had to do the business themselves out on the pitch – they couldn't rely on others!

Further victories over the Faroe Islands (3-0) and Cyprus (2-0), and 1-1 and 2-2 draws with Czechoslovakia, meant that all that stood between Wales and a place in the finals of the greatest football tournament ever was Romania, who they had to beat by at least two goals in their final group game in Cardiff on 7 November to join the Republic of Ireland in America.

Unfortunately for Wales, and of course for Ryan Giggs, Romania spoiled the party and 40,000 fans went home disappointed as their team lost 2-1. It could have been totally different, however. With the scores level at 1-1, Paul Bodin had the chance to give his country the lead but missed from the penalty spot. Romania had taken the lead in the 13th minute, but Dean Saunders equalised on the hour before Florin Radicioiu snatched a dramatic winner with 7 minutes remaining, his second goal of the game.

Romania won the group on goal difference ahead of Belgium (fifteen points each). The Czechs finished third on thirteen points ahead of Wales, fourth with twelve points. It was so close yet so far.

10

Oldham Athletic 2 Manchester United 5
Premier League
29 November 1993

Having lost only once (1-0 at Chelsea) in their first twenty-two Premier League games of the season, United were 'on fire' and victory over Lancashire neighbours Oldham Athletic would extend their lead at the top of the table to an impressive fourteen points.

Manager Alex Ferguson was without Mark Hughes at Boundary Park, bringing Andrei Kanchelskis in his place – and it was the Ukrainian winger who was the star of the show as United scored five times against the plucky Latics, who gave an excellent account of themselves, especially in the first half, despite their lowly League position (eighteenth).

Almost 17,000 fans – Oldham's biggest at home since their stadium was made into an all-seater – certainly got value for money, prompting manager Joe Royle to say: 'We gave it our best shot, but United are a very good side ... they'll win the championship by a mile.'

Oldham Athletic (4-5-1): Hallworth; Fleming, Halle, Jobson, Makin, Bernard, Pedersen, Milligan, Graham (Adams), Holden, Sharpe.
Manchester United (4-5-1): Schmeichel; Parker, Bruce, Pallister, Irwin, Ince (Robson), Kanchelskis, Cantona, Keane, Sharpe, Giggs.
Attendance: 16,708

After a tentative opening, during which time Eric Cantona had a shot saved by Jon Hallworth, United took the lead on 4 minutes.

Cantona found space and slipped in Kanchelskis whose first shot was saved but the winger was quick to react and slotted in the rebound.

Paul Ince then fired wide before former Everton striker Graeme Sharpe cracked in an equaliser on 15 minutes after Denis Irwin had failed miserably to clear his lines.

United came again and, after a clever passing movement, Kanchelskis raced clear in the 18th minute, only to be brought crashing down inside the area. Up stepped the cool-headed Cantona to beat Hallworth with a well-placed spot kick.

In the 26th minute it was level-pegging once more and the unfortunate Irwin was again at fault, committing a foul near the left-hand corner flag. Ex-Manchester City winger Rick Holden took the free kick and beat Schmeichel with a high drive which dipped under the crossbar. Did he intend to score? Holden quietly said afterwards: 'Yes, course I did.'

United responded and, from a quick throw out by Schmeichel, Ryan Giggs raced through only for his shot to be saved by Hallworth. From the resulting corner, delivered by Irwin, centre-back Steve Bruce rose high to head United back in front in the 39th minute.

Oldham battled on; Sharpe and Holden both went close, but on 53 minutes United established a two-goal lead. The outstanding Cantona sent Giggs through and, after checking his run, the Welshman's right-foot shot flew into the net off Richard Jobson's leg. Lucky, yes, but Giggs deserved to score – he was playing superbly.

And there was more to come. Following a 59th minute foul on Paul Parker, Cantona swung over the free-kick, Lee Sharpe headed the ball back across goal towards Roy Keane and Giggs and it was the latter who got the final touch to claim his second goal of the evening and his seventh of the season.

Late on, Schmeichel pulled off a fine save from Paul Bernard while United substitute Brian McClair went close with a header.

This win was United's seventeenth Premier League win of the season. They were in superb form, which was to continue right through until the end of the campaign, culminating with the League and FA Cup double.

11

Manchester United 1 Aston Villa 3
League Cup Final
27 March 1994

With a great chance of completing an historic treble – the Premier League title, FA Cup and League Cup – Manchester United were red-hot favourites with the bookies to beat Aston Villa at Wembley in this, their fourth appearance in the League Cup final.

Romping away at the top of the Premier League and set to play Oldham Athletic in the semi-final of the FA Cup, manager Alex Ferguson was upbeat when he told reporters:

I will be able to field my strongest side and I am confident we will win. We've already beaten Villa twice in the League this season and we are in excellent form right now. But I know from experience that anything can happen in a football match. We will have to be on our guard and I hope it will be a terrific game.

In contrast, Villa boss and former United chief Ron Atkinson said: 'We'll go out and enjoy the occasion. I know United are a good side, but so are we at times!'

On their way to the final, United had knocked out Stoke City, Leicester City, Everton, Portsmouth (in a replay) and Sheffield Wednesday, while Villa had eliminated arch-rivals Birmingham City, Sunderland, Arsenal and Tottenham Hotspur, both away, and Tranmere Rovers, 5-4 on penalties in the semis.

Prior to the Wembley showdown, Villa had lost three Premier League games on the bounce while United were unbeaten in three and, in fact, had lost only two domestic matches all season, both against Chelsea.

Aston Villa (4-5-1): Bosnich; Barrett, McGrath, Teale, Staunton (Cox), Atkinson, Fenton, Richardson, Townsend, Daley; Saunders.
Manchester Utd (4-4-2): Sealey; Parker, Bruce (McClair), Pallister, Irwin; Kanchelskis, Keane, Ince, Giggs (Sharpe); Cantona, Hughes.
Attendance: 77,231

Unfortunately for United there was to be no historic treble. They failed to produce the goods against a well-drilled and sublimely organised Villa side and it was ex-manager Ron Atkinson who celebrated by filling the cup with fizzy stuff after an excellent 3-1 victory.

So for Fergie, Ryan Giggs and the rest of the men in red, it was one down, two to go and now everyone had to concentrate on the real thing – winning the coveted League and FA Cup double.

This defeat was demoralising for United, who were outwitted in one of the best League Cup finals for many years.

Big Ron, who had a huge reputation for getting things right on the day, was spot on tactic-wise, his game plan proving to be a masterstroke.

He knew that United's wingers were potential match-winners, and chose to station Tony Daley and Dalian Atkinson in front of his two full-backs to provide an extra line of defence.

Something similar had worked when Atkinson's Sheffield Wednesday team beat United in the final of the same competition three years earlier, and this time the ploy met with such success that Giggs suffered the rare indignity of being substituted.

The Villa defence was not at all negative and Earl Barrett, who did a superb job in subduing Giggs, regularly found time to get forward down the right.

United started well enough, and early on Eric Cantona picked out Giggs, but the Welshman's header drifted tantalisingly wide. Mark Hughes then went close after Giggs had created the chance with a jinking run.

At times Villa came under intense pressure, but they stuck in there with grim determination. Unable to make their usual progress on the flanks, United tried their luck by going through the middle, but with hard-working midfielder Kevin Richardson fighting for every ball and centre-halves Paul McGrath (ex-United of course) and Shaun Teale rock steady, the route to goal was blocked time and again.

Roy Keane set up Mark Hughes, who should have done better with a close-range header. His miss proved costly when Villa took the lead in the 25th minute with their first attack of any consequence.

Andy Townsend's pass found its way to Dalian Atkinson via Dean Saunders, and the striker took aim before steering the ball past Les Sealey with the outside of his right foot.

Paul Parker, from fully 25 yards, and Gary Pallister, from much closer in, almost grabbed an equaliser while Teale dispossessed Kanchelskis with the sort of heroic last-ditch tackle that inspires everyone.

Villa were defending stubbornly; United were attacking as best they could. And early in the second half Saunders almost made it 2-0, while at the same time Cantona and Giggs came close to scoring at the other end of the pitch.

Villa were frustrating United and, after a rather negative 20-minute spell at the start of the second half, a disconsolate Giggs gave way to Lee Sharpe.

As United pushed forward, so Villa's back line held firm and with 14 minutes remaining they increased their lead. Daley's lightning pace forced Parker to concede a free kick on the edge of the penalty area. Richardson drove the ball hard and low into the danger zone where Saunders used his predatory instincts to net his fourteenth goal of the season with a volley which was all about placement rather than power.

Game over? Not quite. Hughes headed over from 6 yards before giving United a lifeline when he turned smartly on Keane's shot to direct the ball into the far corner of Mark Bosnich's net.

There were 8 minutes left and United had to go for it. On came Brian McClair, for Steve Bruce, and it was all-out attack as Villa back-pedalled and only a remarkable one-handed save by Bosnich prevented Hughes from equalising.

That, however, was it for United and the game was settled in the last minute when Pontypridd referee Keith Cooper, who had an excellent match, had no option but to brandish a red card to United's Ukrainian winger Andrei Kanchelskis, who clearly handled Atkinson's goal-bound follow-up shot after Daley had struck an upright.

As Kanchelskis trudged off, Saunders stepped up to thump the penalty hard and true past Sealey. Villa had won, against the odds, and all credit to United boss Ferguson who said after the game: 'Congratulations to Ron Atkinson; his plan worked well. We weren't at our best.'

Kanchelskis was automatically suspended from United's FA Cup semi-final with Oldham, as were two more key players, Eric Cantona and Roy Keane.

12

Manchester United 4 Oldham Athletic 1
FA Cup Semi-Final Replay
13 April 1994

A crowd of 56,399 had witnessed a 1-1 draw between the two teams at Wembley three days earlier when Mark Hughes cancelled out Neil Pointon's goal with a dramatic equaliser in the last minute of extra time. This time the replay was staged at Maine Road and it was United who came out on top, winning as they equalled Arsenal's record by reaching their twelfth FA Cup final.

Having beaten Sheffield United, Norwich City, Wimbledon and Charlton Athletic in previous rounds, United had been expected (by most) to defeat the Latics at the first attempt, but it was not to be as Joe Royle's team proved tough opponents. Indeed, the Latics had already knocked out Derby County, Stoke City, Barnsley and Bolton Wanderers and although they were struggling at the wrong end of the Premier League table – heading for relegation in fact – they proved resilient to the last.

Kanchelskis and Keane both returned for United (after missing the first game) while Oldham were unchanged with former Old Trafford striker Andy Ritchie on the bench.

Manchester United (4-1-4-1): Schmeichel; Parker, Bruce, Pallister, Irwin, Robson, Ince, Keane (McClair), Giggs, Kanchelskis, Hughes (Sharpe).
Oldham Athletic (4-4-2): Hallworth; Fleming, Jobson, Makin, Pointon (Redmond), Henry, Milligan, Bernard, Holden, Beckford (Ritchie), Sharpe.
Attendance: 32,211

United, who had already scored nine goals in three games against the Latics earlier in the season, including 5-2 and 3-2 victories in the Premier League, began brightly with Bryan Robson, starting his first game since New Year's Day, having the first effort on goal.

And it was the England midfielder who set up United's opening goal on 10 minutes. He fed former Latics star Denis Irwin with an excellent pass and, taking the ball on his chest, the left-back drilled a fierce right-foot shot past Jon Hallworth from 12 yards.

With Oldham on the defensive, United doubled their lead in the 15th minute. Andrei Kanchelskis, out towards the right wing, cut inside and charged across the edge of the penalty area before unleashing a fine left-foot drive which flew past the diving Hallworth.

Oldham hit back and might well have won a penalty after a scrimmage inside the United 18-yard box. Soon afterwards, Darren Beckford came within inches of getting on the end of Graeme Sharpe's forward pass.

After a series of goalmouth incidents at both ends of the field, Oldham got back into the game 5 minutes before half-time.

Robson gave away a corner and from the left-wing flag kick Pointon darted forward to tuck the ball home from close range. In Oldham's next attack, Beckford, well placed, shot straight at Schmeichel.

Early in the second half Curtis Fleming blocked a goal-bound shot from Mark Hughes and Giggs had an effort saved by Hallworth.

United, however, moved up a gear and in the 62nd minute they scored a third goal. Fleming gave away a corner, delivered by Giggs onto the head of the onrushing Robson, who had the easy task of finding the net from 4 yards.

6 minutes later Giggs got on the scoresheet himself as United went 4-1 up. Collecting a pass on the left side of the penalty area, he saw his first shot blocked by Chris Makin but reacted quickly to fire the rebound home with his left foot from 10 yards.

Former United star Ritchie came close late on but it was United's night as they qualified for yet another Cup final.

After the win, the reporter for MANUTD.COM stated, 'The Latics are sliced and diced. United's mojo is well and truly restored in a one-sided display'.

13

Manchester 4 Chelsea 0
FA Cup Final
14 May 1994

For United this was their twelfth appearance in the FA Cup final; for Chelsea it was their fourth.

Both managers were able to field their strongest line-ups and, with United having already been crowned Premier League champions, the Reds were chasing the coveted domestic double for the first time in the club's history. Only five other teams had achieved this feat – Preston North End (1889), Aston Villa (1897), Tottenham Hotspur (1961), Arsenal (1971) and Liverpool (1986).

Chelsea had finished a disappointing fourteenth in the Premier League but they had beaten United in both home and away games. United, meanwhile, were bang in form, having lost only six times in open play all season.

Chelsea (4-4-2): Kharine; Clarke, Sinclair, Kjeldberg, Johnson, Burley (Hoddle), Spencer, Newton, Stein (Cascarino), Peacock, Wise.
Manchester United (4-4-1-1): Schmeichel; Parker, Bruce, Pallister, Irwin (Sharpe), Kanchelskis (McClair), Keane, Ince, Giggs, Cantona, Hughes.
Attendance: 79,634

Referee David Elleray (Harrow) was in charge of the final – and as you will read he made a big mistake halfway through the second half!

The opening 45 minutes weren't great. Chelsea perhaps were the better team with both Stein and Peacock having decent chances. In contrast, United looked nervous at times and their midfield trio of Paul Ince, Roy Keane and wide man Andrei Kanchelskis found it tough against the hard-tackling Londoners.

Things, however, changed dramatically after the interval. Following 15 minutes of tentative play, during which time Mark Hughes came close for United and Gavin Peacock likewise for Chelsea, referee Elleray – 4 yards away from the incident – awarded United a penalty on the hour when Eddie Newton clattered into Denis Irwin as the full-back collected Ryan Giggs' pass and charged into the area.

The cool-headed Eric Cantona strolled up to send Moscow-born goalkeeper Dmitri Kharine the wrong way with a majestic side-footed spot-kick, making him the first Frenchman to play (and indeed score) in an FA Cup final, while at the same time Kharine became the first Russian to appear in a final.

8 minutes later United were awarded a second penalty when Frank Sinclair was adjudged to have fouled Kanchelskis as he raced into the 18-yard box. And once again cool dude Cantona delivered, slotting the ball home precisely into the same corner as his first spot kick.

A stunned Chelsea tried all they could to get back into the game, but in the 68th minute it was virtually game over when Mark Hughes raced through in the inside-right position to drill home United's third goal ... his fourth in as many games at Wembley during the season.

Chelsea didn't lie down and United's goalkeeper Peter Schmeichel made two smart saves to deny Peacock and John Spencer while Dennis Wide fired inches wide.

Then, with time fast running out and Chelsea's defence all at sea, Paul Ince made ground down the left and after rounding a stranded Kharine he unselfishly rolled the ball into Brian McClair's path for the substitute to score the easiest goal of his career to give United a 4-0 victory.

After the game, referee Elleray admitted publicly that 'he got it wrong when awarding United a second penalty.' He was 30 yards or so away from the incident and although he made the wrong decision he got no help whatsoever from his linesman!

Manchester United 2 Blackburn Rovers 0
FA Charity Shield
14 August 1994

Back at Wembley for the third time in 1994, and looking to lift the annual Charity Shield outright for a record eighth time and for the tenth time overall, United were also hoping to win their third trophy of the year, following success in the FA Cup final.

Blackburn, who were managed by Kenny Dalglish, finished runners-up to the Reds in the Premier League and on paper looked to have a strong squad of players.

However, there were two notable absentees from their side – top scorer Alan Shearer and his strike partner Chris Sutton, who had just joined the Ewood Park club for a national record fee of £5 million. Tony Gale was handed his Rovers debut by Dalglish, who also named his young forward Peter Thorne as a substitute.

United boss Alex Ferguson had no real selection problems, but he was without Roy Keane and gave defender David May his first game for the club just weeks after he had moved to Old Trafford from Blackburn for £1.4 million. Nicky Butt and Dion Dublin were among the substitutes.

Blackburn Rovers (4-4-1-1): Flowers; Berg, Hendrey, Gale, Le Saux, Slater, Atkins (Thorne), Sherwood, Wilcox, Ripley, Pearce.
Manchester United (3-4-2-1): Schmeichel; May, Bruce, Pallister, Sharpe, Kanchelskis, McClair, Ince, Giggs, Cantona, Hughes.
Attendance: 60,402

In bright sunshine, Middlesex referee Philip Don got the game up and running and it was United who threatened early on with Mark Hughes producing a terrific left-handed save by Rovers' goalkeeper Tim Flowers.

Soon afterwards Hughes saw another well-struck effort again saved by Flowers, this time using his right hand.

With Rovers pinned back in their own half, it came as no surprise when United took the lead on 22 minutes. Paul Ince, who was having a fine game, drove into the penalty area only to be floored by Rovers' centre-back Colin Hendrey.

Penalty … and up stepped French ace Eric Cantona to nonchalantly stroke home the spot kick, sending Flowers the wrong way. This was his third penalty conversion at Wembley in the space of four months.

Blackburn, to their credit, responded and ex-Chelsea man Ian Pearce had a chance to equalise from a cross by another former Stamford Bridge favourite, Graeme Le Saux, but he mistimed his header which flew high and wide of Peter Schmeichel's goal.

United went in at the break having had 65 per cent of the play. They looked comfortable but Rovers were still in with a shout.

Early in the second half, the lively Andrei Kanchelskis fired over from Ryan Giggs' low centre into the box, before Giggs himself, after a mazy dribble down the left when he turned Henning Berg inside out, was unlucky with a cross shot which flew a yard wide of Flowers' far post.

Blackburn replied and Pearce, left free inside the area, should have equalised but somehow managed to screw his shot high and wide of the United goal (it looked as if the ball had gone off his shin).

United picked up their game as the minutes rolled by and, after a couple of close shaves, they secured victory with a truly magnificent second goal with 9 minutes remaining.

May won a corner on the right. Giggs delivered the flag kick, Cantona headed on and upwards towards the penalty spot where Ince, back to goal, met the ball perfectly with a stunning overhead kick. Great stuff … and it effectively sewed up victory for the Reds.

Hughes had two more efforts at goal late on as Rovers tired, and when the final whistle sounded there were celebrations aplenty for Giggs and his ecstatic teammates, the majority of whom collected another medal to add to their growing tallies.

Referee Philip Don handed out seven yellow cards, four to Rovers players.

For the record, Blackburn went on to have a wonderful season, winning the Premier League title by a point from United (89/88) after Fergie's men could only draw their last game of the campaign at West Ham. Victory at Upton Park would, of course, have given the Reds their third Championship in a row.

15

Manchester United 9 Ipswich Town 0
Premier League
4 March 1995

Seven days prior to what was to be a very one-sided encounter, United had lost 1-0 at Everton, allowing Blackburn Rovers, who were held 0-0 by Norwich City, to increase their lead at the top of the Premier League by one point, from four to five. On the other hand, Ipswich, managed by former player George Burley, were deep in relegation trouble, lying twenty-first in the table and heading fast towards Division One. They had won only six of their thirty League games, struggling to score goals while conceding fifty-eight. Goalkeeper Craig Forrest had managed only one clean sheet all season.

Earlier in the campaign United had surprisingly lost 3-2 at Portman Road, so this was a match when revenge was the name of the game, with manager Ferguson naming what he believed was certainly his strongest team, with Roy Keane and Denis Irwin selected in the two full-back positions.

Prior to this match, the two teams had met fifty-one times in all competitions, with United having the upper hand with twenty-five wins to Ipswich's eighteen. The Tractormen had only netted once in their last six visits to Old Trafford, winning there in 1983/84.

Manchester United (4-4-2): Schmeichel; Keane (Sharpe), Bruce (Butt), Pallister, Irwin, Kanchelskis, Ince, Giggs, McClair, Cole, Hughes.
Ipswich Town (4-4-2): Forrest; Yallop, Wark, Linighan, Thompson, Palmer, Williams, Sedgley, Slater, Chapman (Marshall), Mathie.
Attendance: 43,804

Graham Poll from Berkshire was the match referee and he would spent most of the game patrolling Ipswich Town's half of the field!

United started off like a house on fire and, after a couple of strong attacks, they shot into the lead on 15 minutes. Irwin's throw in found Mark Hughes, who laid the ball across the edge of the penalty area to Roy Keane, who netted with a crisp, low drive past Forrest's right hand.

With the sun out, and United on a mission, Ryan Giggs darted down the left wing like a whippet, and from his measured cross Andy Cole swooped to net number two.

Soon afterwards Keane was a yard away from making it 3-0 while, at the other end, ex-Newcastle forward Alex Mathie should have reduced the deficit but hesitated and his shot was blocked.

In the 37th minute United scored their third goal. A terrific overhead kick by Hughes smacked against the Ipswich crossbar and when the ball came down Cole simply couldn't miss, slipping home his second of the afternoon.

With Ipswich now firmly under the cosh, Brian McClair was unlucky when he tried a similar overhead kick moments later.

The second half was only 8 minutes old when United went four-nil ahead. Irwin (on the right this time) drilled the ball high into the danger zone, where Cole jumped above John Wark to steer his header wide of Forrest and so complete his first hat-trick for the Reds while, at the same time, taking his goal-tally to seven goals in his first seven appearances for the club.

2 minutes later the impressive Giggs raced away (yet again) down the left flank and with the Ipswich defence all at sea, his low, precise cross to the far post was met by Hughes. Bang – five-nil.

95 seconds on from that, United almost bagged a sixth goal when Andrei Kanchelskis scampered clear down the Ipswich left, crossed to Cole and whose shot was blocked. Reprieve for Ipswich? No, not really. 2 minutes later, Forrest did well to thwart Giggs but, as the ball diverted upwards, Hughes leapt highest to find the net to make if half-a-dozen for the rampant Reds.

'We want seven,' chanted the fans ... and their wish was granted on 65 minutes when Cole exchanged passes with Hughes before slamming home his fourth goal of the afternoon. The entire Ipswich team looked totally demoralised and it got worse! After Hughes had almost split the crossbar with a booming drive, United claimed an eighth goal in bizarre circumstances.

With his defenders all at sea, Ipswich keeper Forrest raced out of his goal in attempt to clear his lines, but in doing so handled the ball well outside the penalty area. Referee Poll blew up for a foul and booked Forrest, but before the keeper could get back into position Hughes played a quick free-kick to Ince who took aim and netted from fully 40 yards.

United kept up the pressure and with 3 minutes remaining Giggs, who was outstanding throughout, set Ince up for a header which found its way to Cole, who cleverly turned his marker before smashing in his fifth goal of the game to sew up a convincing and comprehensive nine-nil victory for United.

A gum-chewing Alex Ferguson said afterwards, 'Wow that was some win. Didn't we play well? I feel sorry for Ipswich; they were simply no match for my players.'

* This was United's second biggest 'League' win in the club's 103-year history (playing under Newton Heath, they had beaten Wolverhampton Wanderers 10-1 in

October 1892). And it was only one goal short of their best-ever win (in terms of goal-difference) in all competitions, having crushed RSC Anderlecht 10-0 in a preliminary round second leg European Cup game in September 1956.

- This 9-0 victory over Ipswich, however, is still the biggest victory in Premier League football (since 1992).
- Andy Cole's five-timer was a Premier League record at the time, later equalled by Newcastle's Alan Shearer *v.* Sheffield Wednesday in September 1999 Tottenham's Jermain Defoe against Wigan Athletic in November 2009 and Manchester City's Sergio Aguero against Newcastle in October 2015.
- And this drubbing for Ipswich was their heaviest at League level, and was one goal short of their worst-ever defeat, 10-1 at Fulham on Boxing Day 1963.

16

Manchester United 4 Southampton 1
Premier League
18 November 1995

Southampton had won only one of their previous sixteen competitive games against United and they knew that their overall record at Old Trafford was not at all good, having last won on the ground in 1988.

Indeed, the Saints had not been marching too well ahead of this Premier League game! They were languishing in fifteenth position in the table, although they had won their last two games, beating Wimbledon 2-1 and QPR 2-0.

In contrast, United were lying second, behind Newcastle United, and had lost only two of their opening twelve League games, including a 1-0 reverse at Arsenal a fortnight earlier.

Old Trafford's biggest crowd of the season at the time – well over 39,000 – turned out to see manager Alex Ferguson name an unchanged team, while Saints' boss Dave Merrington was missing the influential figure of Matt Le Tissier.

Manchester United (4-4-2): Schmeichel; G. Neville, Bruce, Pallister, Irwin (P. Neville), Beckham, Butt, Scholes (McClair), Cantona, Giggs (Sharpe), Cole.
Southampton (4-4-1-1): Beasant; Dodd, Hall, Monkou, Benali, Hughes, Widdrington, Magilton, Heaney (Bennett), Watson (Maddison), Shipperley.
Attendance: 39,301

15 seconds after referee Paul Danson got the game started, United scored through Ryan Giggs. It seemed as if the Saints' defenders were still asking each other who should mark who when Paul Scholes collected a misplaced pass and drove a 40-yard ball out to Eric Cantona on the left. The Frenchman checked his stride, cut inside and slipped in the on-rushing Giggs who scored with a low left-footed drive past Dave Beasant from near the penalty spot.

This remains to this day (2015) the fastest goal ever scored by a Manchester United player in a first-class match.

Amazingly, with spectators still entering the ground, Giggs made it two-nil in the 4th minute and 90 seconds later Paul Scholes put United three-nil ahead … game over!

Southampton looked shell-shocked and, although they recovered after that early blitz by United, they never really threatened Peter Schmeichel's goal.

United, in fact, had the majority of possession but some dogged defending by the visitors kept them at bay until Andy Cole bagged a fourth goal halfway through the second half ... 3 minutes after Ferguson had denied Giggs his hat-trick by substituting him with Lee Sharpe.

With 5 minutes remaining, the former Chelsea striker Neil Shipperley netted a consolation for Saints, but by this time United were strolling, having wrapped up the points with that devastating early charge which produced three goals in 6 minutes.

As it was, Southampton battled on and avoided relegation on goal difference ahead of Manchester City, who slipped Division One along with QPR and Bolton. United went from strength to strength, overhauled Newcastle and went on to win the title, again.

These are the fastest goals scored in Premier League football (at 2015):

10.0 secs.	Ledley King for Tottenham Hotspur *v.* Bradford City, 2000
10.4 secs.	Alan Shearer for Newcastle United *v.* Manchester City, 2003
11.1 secs.	Mark Viduka for Leeds United *v.* Charlton Athletic, 2001
13.0 secs.	Chris Sutton for Blackburn Rovers *v.* Everton, 1995
13.0 secs.	Dwight Yorke for Aston Villa *v.* Coventry City, 1995
13.0 secs.	Asmir Begovic for Stoke City v. Southampton, 2013
14.0 secs.	Jesus Navas for Manchester City *v.* Tottenham Hotspur, 2013
15.0 secs.	Ryan Giggs for Manchester United *v.* Southampton, 1995

17

Manchester United 3 Middlesbrough 0
Premier League
5 May 1996

The scene was set ... and everyone associated with Manchester United knew they had to get something (a point at least) in this match, their final Premier League game of the season, against twelfth-placed Middlesbrough at the Riverside Stadium, to win the title for the third time in four years.

Defeat could see them finish second in the table behind Newcastle if the Geordies defeated Tottenham Hotspur at St James' Park.

Going into their final weekend of games, the top of the division looked like this:

1. *Manchester United on 79 points, goal difference + 35*
2. *Newcastle United on 77 points, goal difference + 29*

The Reds were on an excellent run, having lost only once in their previous thirteen Premier League games (1-0 at Southampton), while Newcastle were undefeated in four but had also lost four of their last ten matches, allowing United to overtake them and become firm favourites to win the championship.

Alex Ferguson brought back Nicky Butt in midfield and named both Steve Bruce and Andy Cole on the bench, while former Old Trafford hero Bryan Robson, now in charge of Middlesbrough, named an unchanged team with the emphasis on attack. Ex-United keeper Gary Walsh was between the posts.

Ryan Giggs, in a pre-match interview, said, 'This will be a tough game. Middlesbrough have nothing to lose and everything to gain. We will have to be at our best, be professional and I believe we'll win. But it will be close.'

Middlesbrough (4-4-2): Walsh; Cox, Vickers, Pearson, Whyte, Branco, Barmby, Pollock (Stamp), Mustoe, Juninho, Fjortoft.
Manchester United (4-4-2): Schmeichel; Irwin, Pallister, P. Neville, May, Beckham, Keane, Butt, Scholes (Cole), Cantona, Giggs.
Attendance: 29,922

Tension inside the stadium was electric and with almost 2,500 fans behind them it was United, in their change strip of broad blue and white shirts and matching shorts, who got into their stride fastest, with Eric Cantona and David Beckham in the thick of the action.

Gary Pallister, playing against his former club, cleared his lines following 'Boro's first worthwhile attack before United took the lead to relieve the pressure.

Winning a corner on the right flank, Ryan Giggs swung over the flag-kick left-footed to the far post where the on-rushing David May rose highest to send his downward header past Walsh and high into the net on the bounce for his first goal of the season.

United kept up the momentum and both Cantona and Scholes went close, as did the Brazilian Juninho for 'Boro who were resilient to the last, challenging for every ball and giving United's plenty to think about.

As the players left the pitch at half-time, news filtered through that Newcastle were being held 0-0 by Spurs, and when play resumed after the interval United went for the jugular. And they were rewarded with a second goal in the 54th minute, courtesy of substitute Andy Cole, who had been introduced into the action seconds earlier.

The impressive Giggs whipped over another left-wing corner, and after the ball was nudged into the middle of the danger zone, there was Cole, turning superbly to find the net with a clever shot for his eleventh Premier League goal of the season.

3 minutes later, with the United fans celebrating, word got round that Spurs had taken the lead at St James' Park. It was all over bar the shouting and, although Les Ferdinand equalised for Newcastle, Ryan Giggs crowned a superb display by cracking in a third goal for United from 22 yards in the 81st minute after some neat work on the left by Butt.

1. Ryan Giggs in action during the friendly match between Singha All Star XI and Manchester United at Rajamangala Stadium on 13 July 2013 in Thailand. (mooinblack/Shutterstock.com)

2. Ryan Giggs during the warm-up for the match PSV v. Manchester United at the Philips Stadium, in Eindhoven, the Netherlands, on 14 September 2015. (kayintveen/Shutterstock.com)

4. Ryan Giggs, again during the Singha All Star XI *v.* Manchester United friendly at Rajamangala Stadium. (mooinblack/Shutterstock.com)

5. Barcelona midfielder Javier Mascherano and Ryan Giggs during the 2011 UEFA Champions League final between Manchester United and FC Barcelona (28 May 2011). (Mitch Gunn/Shutterstock.com)

6. Ryan Giggs (*left*) and Michael Carrick (*right*) during team warm-ups before a friendly match against Malaysia at the National Stadium on 17 July 2009 in Kuala Lumpur. (Jaggat Rashidi/Shutterstock.com)

7. Ryan Giggs during the Manchester United first-team training pre-season tour of Bangkok at Rajmalanga Stadium on on 12 July 2013 in Bangkok, Thailand. (Rnoid/ Shutterstock.com)

8. Manchester United v. Bolton at Old Trafford, 17 October 2009 in Manchester. (Marius Wigen/Shutterstock.com)

18

Manchester United 1 Liverpool 0
FA Cup Final
11 May 1996

As you've read, a few days before the final United had secured their third Premier League title in four years, 1993, 1994 and 1996, and finished second in 1995. The final against Liverpool was also their third in three seasons, having beaten Chelsea 4-0 in 1994 and lost 1-0 to Everton in 1995.

The Merseyside club, on the other hand, were going through a barren spell in terms of trophies, having not won a League championship since 1990 or the FA Cup since 1992, although they had tasted League Cup glory in 1995.

At the time of the Wembley showdown, Liverpool and United had been the two top-scoring sides in the Premier League, and went into the game as the most attacking sides in English football, with Liverpool winning the last meeting between the two clubs by 2-0 at Anfield while the fixture at Old Trafford had ended in a 2-2 draw.

Robbie Fowler had scored all four of those Liverpool goals in the Premier League and United manager Alex Ferguson, gritting, said, 'If we can stop Fowler, we'll win the Cup.'

Liverpool (5-2-1-2): James; McAteer, Scales, Wright, Babb, Jones (Thomas), McManaman, Redknapp, Barnes, Collymore (Rush), Fowler.
Manchester United (4-4-1-1): Schmeichel; Irwin, P. Neville, Pallister, May, Keane, Beckham (G. Neville), Butt, Giggs, Cantona, Cole (Scholes).
Attendance: 79,007

To be truthful, the match itself, despite the rivalry between the two teams, was a fairly unmemorable game, rarely sparking into life, with playmakers Eric Cantona and Steve McManaman marked and closed out by Jamie Redknapp and John Barnes and Roy Keane and Nicky Butt respectively.

The impressive Keane stopped virtually every attack the Liverpool midfield threw at United, and as commentator Peter Brackley described, 'covered every blade of grass'. The Irishman comfortably won the 'Man of the Match' award ... he was outstanding.

The game started at a frenetic pace with United looking the more positive, and in fact they created a couple of early chances, David Beckham – set up by Ryan Giggs – seeing one terrific drive saved by James, before Liverpool gradually clawed themselves back into the game with Redknapp firing over after some trickery on the left by McManaman.

However, chances at either end were somewhat limited. Neither of the two goalkeepers, Peter Schmeichel for United and David James for Liverpool, were seriously tested throughout the majority of the game. Schmeichel was perhaps the busier of the two, but he only had to deal with crosses into the danger zone and only twice had to drop onto the lush turf.

With just 5 minutes remaining on Oxford referee Dermot Gallagher's watch, and with extra-time looming, United won a corner on the right. Beckham floated the ball into the crowded area. Keeper James, under pressure from Gary Pallister, attempted to get distance on his punch but only succeeded in sending the ball a yard outside the penalty box, to the feet of United's captain Cantona.

The Frenchman, who had scored for United in the 2-2 draw at Old Trafford earlier in the season – his comeback game after a seven-week layoff – drew back his right foot before sending his shot screaming goalwards, through the crowded penalty area and into the back of the Liverpool net. Great joy, great celebrations.

Prior to the 85th minute, Cantona had been marked out of the game. In fact, he had managed only three attempts on target all afternoon, one producing a fine save from James, but true to his form all season he popped up with yet another magical moment with his nineteenth and most crucial goal of the campaign.

There was no way back for the Merseysiders as United comfortably held out to lift the Cup for a record ninth time in the club's history. It was also United's third FA Cup triumph under manager Alex Ferguson while, at the same time, the Reds also became first club to complete the double (League and FA Cup) on two occasions.

Liverpool boss Roy Evans congratulated United, saying, 'They were just that much better on the day, but to lose so late on was hard to take.'

In contrast, Ryan Giggs – for whom it was his 241st competitive appearance for the club – said after collecting his second FA Cup winner's medal, 'I'm delighted. It was another memorable occasion for me and indeed for the rest of the team, and it took another terrific strike from King Eric to win a tight game.'

N.B. Two notable absentees from the United side were the club's two longest serving players Steve Bruce and Brian McClair, who were left out, David May and Paul Scholes replacing them. Bruce never played for United again, being transferred to Birmingham City eleven days after the final, while McClair remained at the club for a further two seasons and added another Premier League winner's medal to his collection.

19

Manchester United 5 Sunderland 0
Premier League
21 December 1996

Going into this game, reigning Premier League champions United, unbeaten in five games, were lying sixth in the table while Sunderland, fresh from a 3-0 home win over Chelsea, were stationed in fourteenth position.

During the first half of the season United boss Alex Ferguson, despite seeing his defence concede five goals at Newcastle and six at Southampton, had kept faith with at least six players, namely Peter Schmeichel, Denis Irwin, David May, Eric Cantona, David Beckham, Ole Gunnar Solskjaer and Ryan Giggs, but at the same time he had already used a total of twenty-two by the time Sunderland set foot inside Old Trafford.

Giggs had been in good form, so too had Cantona and Solskjaer, while Schmeichel, had performed well between the posts as usual, although twenty-eight goals had already gone past him in all competitions.

Manchester United (5-3-2): Schmeichel; G. Neville, Pallister (McClair), May, Irwin, P. Neville, Butt, Scholes, Giggs (Thornley), Cantona, Solskjaer (Poborsky).
Sunderland: Perez; Kubicki, Hall, Ord, Melville, Gray (Bridges), Ball, Rae (Stewart, Bracewell (Agnew), Kelly, Russell.
Attendance: 55,081

Eric Cantona was quite brilliant in this game, so too was Ryan Giggs!

The Frenchman – in his final season with United – scored a stunning goal, the fifth, with a sublime chip to seal what in the end turned out to be a comfortable victory, their biggest of the season.

Cantona also netted from the penalty spot in the first half, but in effect the visitors made the brighter start in this, the first Premier League meeting between the clubs.

Unfortunately the Wearsiders could not find the back of the United net and they were punished in the 35th minute when United took the lead.

After taking a pass from Phil Neville, Giggs, lively and impish, and hugging the touchline, crossed hard and low from the left to Paul Scholes, whose well-struck volley was parried by Sunderland goalkeeper Lionel Perez, only for Ole Gunnar Solskjaer, alert as ever, to head home his seventh goal of the season from 8 yards out to give the reigning double-winners the edge.

Sunderland, playing in unfamiliar white shirts and black shorts, battled well and twice went close to equalising but 2 minutes before the interval they fell two behind.

Giggs once again crossed from the left; Scholes' delivered a forward pass to send Nicky Butt charging into the 18-yard box and, as the midfielder rounded Perez, so the French goalkeeper brought him down. A clear penalty, said referee Paul Durkin. Up stepped the cool-headed, and Perez's fellow countryman, Cantona to send Perez the wrong way from the spot and so double United's lead.

The floodgates really opened in the second half and only 3 minutes had passed when Solskjaer made it 3-0 in a swift counter-attack after goalkeeper Peter Schmeichel threw the ball downfield just seconds after making a save. The Norwegian striker actually collected the ball 10 yards inside his own half of the field and ran on virtually unchallenged before beating Perez to his right from just inside the Sunderland penalty area.

Butt headed in a teasing and tempting Giggs left-wing corner in the 58th minute for his second goal in successive home matches to put United four-nil in front before Cantona's moment of glory arrived 10 minutes from time.

Collecting the ball just inside the Sunderland half, he jinked past two bemused opponents with a wonderful piece of skill before running directly at the visiting defence. He then exchanged passes with Brian McClair before lifting the ball over the helpless Perez from the edge of the area. What a brilliant goal – one of the best seen at Old Trafford for many a year.

One reporter wrote, 'Cantona took centre-stage with a sumptuous turn, deft chip and iconic celebration.' And this wonderful effort made the shortlist for the best goal at the Premier League 20 Seasons Awards in 2012.

United in fact dominated the game for the last half-hour and substitute Karel Poborsky (twice), Cantona and Scholes all went close to adding to the scoresheet. Sunderland, to their credit, stuck in there and David Kelly and Paul Stewart both tested Schmeichel to the full.

After the game, Sunderland manager Peter Reid admitted, 'Arguably we were the better side for an hour but goals change games, and in the end we suffered badly because we simply did not take our chances.'

Alex Ferguson said, 'Sunderland played very well for most of the first half. We couldn't get going, but when the second goal went in, there was only going to be one winner – United. And what a terrific goal Cantona scored. It was stunning – one of the best I've ever seen.'

United went on to win the championship in 1996/97, finishing seven points clear of Newcastle. And this was a fitting finale for Cantona who chose to retire at the age of thirty, having played a key role in all four of the Reds' Premier League-winning seasons at Old Trafford.

Unfortunately Sunderland, who were competing in their first-ever season in the Premier League, were relegated, losing top-flight status by a single point.

20

Manchester United 4 FC Porto 0
Champions League, Quarter Final, 1st Leg
5 March 1997

The Portuguese giants – champions of Europe ten years previously – were one of the favourites to win the competition again in 1997, having blasted through the group stage with sixteen points out of a possible eighteen, scoring twelve goals and conceding only four. And they had certainly looked good, very good in fact, especially when beating AC Milan at home and away.

For United, meanwhile, it had been a much harder passage and they eventually progressed from their group with nine points, seven behind Juventus.

For the Porto game, manager Alex Ferguson chose to play two strikers, Andy Cole and Ole Gunnar Solskjaer, and three across the middle, Eric Cantona, David Beckham and Ryan Giggs. Denis Irwin and Gary Neville were his chosen full-backs, Ronny Johnsen and Gary Pallister his two central defenders with David May just in front.

Sitting on top of the Premier League with a sixteen-match unbeaten run behind them, United were confident of gaining a result against their Portuguese opponents. But as a cautious Giggs said before kick-off, 'We treat every game as it comes, and Porto look a very useful team. We will know we will have to be at our best to beat them.'

Manchester United (4-1-3-2): Schmeichel; Irwin, Johnsen, Pallister, May, G. Neville, Beckham, Giggs, Cantona, Cole, Solskjaer.
FC Porto (4-5-1): Hilario; Conceicao, Jorge Costa, Aloisio, Paulinho Santos, Drulovic, Edmilson, Barrosa, Joao Costa (Jardel), Zahovic, Artur (Barros).
Attendance: 53,415

Cynics might have scoffed at such an outrageously risky attacking line-up but Fergie knew what he was doing!

Highly-rated referee Anders Frisk got the game underway and immediately United were on the offensive, but it was Porto who threatened first and only a smothering left-footed save by Peter Schmeichel from the Brazilian Artur kept the visitors at bay.

United then clicked into gear, got hold of the ball and pushed their opponents back. The speed with which the red-shirted players got forward and the number involved in almost every attack was quite breathtaking and proved too much for the Porto defence to handle, not to mention the fact that they failed to deal with almost every high ball played into the area.

This unusual frantic, hassling approach from United gave Porto no time whatsoever to play the game they were used to and, but for an Artur 70-second effort, the Portuguese side failed to trouble United's central defence all evening!

David May's instinctive finish on 22 minutes, after Porto keeper Henrique Hilário could only parry Gary Pallister's header, settled the Old Trafford nerves.

Cole then saw a firm header tipped over before Cantona grabbed a second goal on 34 minutes, netting with a firm low right-footed drive from near the penalty spot.

Porto looked disinterested at this point. Some of their players seemed far too relaxed and for long periods it was all United as the men clad in broad blue and white striped shirts ran round chasing shadows!

The torment continued after half-time and when United scored a third goal in the 61st minute, it was effectively game and, indeed, tie over!

The third strike is rated by many as one of the best goals ever seen at Old Trafford.

As Porto pushed forward, in an attempt to get back into the game, substitute Rui Barros sent a left-wing cross into the area; it was far too high and very long. In fact, the ball beat everyone and fell to the feet of Cantona, who was lurking in the left back position.

United fans, young and old, were well aware of the Frenchman's ability, but the pass he then produced is imprinted in the memory of every supporter who was present, and some may never see such a movement ever again.

With the outside of his right boot, Cantona swept a long pass around an onrushing Porto defender and down the left wing. The ball was within inches of going out of play, but somehow it held its line and magically curled back inside for Andy Cole to run onto.

It was an absolute peach of a pass. The Old Trafford crowd was on its feet, urging Cole on, and he granted them their wish, forcing Jorge Costa to back-peddle towards his own penalty area. Everybody expected Cole to go it alone and finish off the move, but suddenly, out of nowhere, Giggs appeared on left side of the edge of the 18-yard box, having made a 60-yard dash to offer Cole an alternative. The striker spotted his colleague and played a short reverse pass into the Welshman's feet, who went on to drill a low, precise shot past the hapless Hilario at his near-post.

The goal itself, the buildup, the execution, was magnificent and it signalled the arrival once again of Manchester United in Europe.

With 10 minutes remaining, 'Man of the Match' Cantona slipped in the tireless Cole who coolly claimed a fourth goal to complete Porto's humiliation.

The return leg would prove a rather dull affair, in comparison, United holding firm to claim a 0-0 draw and book a place in the semi-finals of the competition for the first time in twenty-eight years.

5 March 1997 was, without doubt, the night that heralded United's coming of age and the beginning of a bright new and triumphant future. And the victory over Porto and the build up to Giggs' goal will live in the memories of the United fans forever.

Several people, Fergie, Giggs, Beckham included, did not expect United to beat Porto so easily. In fact, the majority didn't give them a sniff of a chance of getting anything against a very strong side. But as it was, United not only defeated Porto, they annihilated them.

To sum up ... this 4-0 destruction of the Portuguese champions ranks amongst United's greatest ever European victories, certainly one of their best ever at Old Trafford. The return leg ended in a 0-0 draw, but United were never going to lose anyway!

21

Manchester United 0 Borussia Dortmund 1
(United lost 0-2 on aggregate)
Champions League, Semi-Final, 2nd Leg
23 April 1997

Playing in their first Champions League/European Cup semi-final since 1969, Manchester United had lost their first leg encounter with Borussia Dortmund by a goal to nil in front of 48,500 fans, René Tretschok scoring 15 minutes from time, and they knew it would be mighty tough to turn things round in the return game at Old Trafford. The Bundesliga side had one of the best defences in the competition, having conceded only nine goals in nine games – and they had one of the best goalkeepers in the game as well in Stefan Klos.

Managed by Ottmar Hitzfeld, Dortmund had a fairly settled side with Karl-Heinz Riedle, Jorg Heinrich and Lars Ricken in excellent goal-scoring form, while defenders Jürgen Kohler and Wolfgang Feiersinger were two of the best in the business. And they also had Scotsman Paul Lambert in midfield; who would go on to manage Livingston, Wycombe Wanders, Colchester United, Norwich City and Aston Villa.

Prior to meeting the German side in the first leg on 9 April, Premier League leaders United had lost two of their previous four League games. But following that narrow defeat in Dortmund, they won two in succession on the road, at Blackburn and Liverpool, leaving manager Alex Ferguson a dilemma for the return game ... should he bring back Ryan Giggs or not? He chose to leave the Welshman on the bench, but perhaps more importantly he had Peter Schmeichel back in goal and David Beckham returned in midfield.

The other semi-final second leg was between Ajax Amsterdam and Juventus, with the Italian club leading 2-1.

Manchester United (4-1-2-1-2): Schmeichel; G. Neville, May, Pallister, P. Neville (Scholes), Johnsen, Beckham, Butt, Cantona, Solskjaer (Giggs), Cole.
Borussia Dortmund (3-5-2): Klos; Feiersinger, Kree, Kohler, Reuter (Tretschok), Möller, Lambert, Ricken, Heinrich, Riedle, Chapulsat.
Attendance: 53,606

Swiss referee Urs Meier got the game underway and after, David May had gone close for United, the home supporters inside Old Trafford were stunned when Dortmund scored a vital away goal. A passing movement down United's left led to Ricken cutting inside to beat Schmeichel with a low shot to the keeper's right.

This left United with a mountain to climb and they knew it as passes went astray and some clumsy challengers were penalised by the referee.

Andy Cole and Cantona came close to equalising; Cantona, in fact, should have scored, before Ronny Johnsen fired wide and centre-half Gary Pallister headed past Klos's right-hand post when he, too, should have found the net as he was only 6 yards from goal!

United kept plugging away, but Dortmund were dangerous on the break and Schmeichel twice had to be alert to deny Heinrich and Stephane Chapulsat.

United still created – and missed – chances and this led Ferguson into making his first change, bringing on Giggs for Solskjaer in the 57th minute. Immediately he crossed from the wing but saw the usually confident Cantona miss the target. Cole was also guilty of another miss, while Giggs had a good effort saved by Klos.

At the other end of the pitch, Heinrich almost made it 2-0 and it took a splendid tackle from Pallister to thwart Riedle, before Lambert got in on the act with a long-range shot that drifted wide.

But as the minutes ticked away, United seemed to run out of ideas. Dortmund closed the back door and in the end they ran out comfortable winners, leaving Giggs and his teammates totally disappointed.

'We're all gutted,' said Beckham after the game, and Giggs, looking as a sick as a pig, sighed, saying, 'Ah well, there'll be another chance one day.'

N.B. Juventus beat Ajax 4-1 in the other semi-final second leg (6-2 on aggregate) to qualify for the final, which they won, beating United's conquerors Borussia Dortmund 3-1 in Munich.

22

Manchester United 3 Juventus 2
Champions League, Group B
1 October 1997

This was a game where Manchester United felt they could send out a message of intent to Europe ... if they could secure a favourable result against Juventus, who at the time were rated as a great side with top players like the French duo of Zinedine Zidane and Didier Deschamps, Italian maestro Allesandro Del Piero, his fellow countryman Paolo Montero and the South African-born Teixeira Dimas all in their prime.

United had won their opening Group B game against Košice in Slovakia 3-0 and, besides Juventus, they still had to play Dutch champions Feyenoord.

Manager Alex Ferguson, unfortunately without the injured Roy Keane, elected to play ex-Spurs star Teddy Sheringham and Ole Gunnar Solskjaer up front, Ryan Giggs and David Beckham on the flanks and Nicky Butt and Ronny Johnsen in midfield, with Henning Berg in front of the back four.

Manchester United (4-1-3-2): Schmeichel; G. Neville, Pallister, Berg, Irwin, Johnsen, Butt (Scholes), Beckham, Giggs, Sheringham, Solskjaer (P. Neville).
Juventus (4-4-2): Peruzzi; Ferrara, Montero, Pecchia (Iuliano), Dimas, Inghazi, Del Piero (Amoroso), Deschamps, Birindeli, Tacchinardi (Pessotto), Zidane.
Attendance: 53,428

13 seconds after Spanish referee Antonio Lopez Nieto had blown his whistle to start the game, and before hundreds of fans had taken their seats, Juventus stunned Old Trafford, and more so Manchester United, by taking the lead through Del Piero. This is one of the quickest goals ever scored at Old Trafford.

Once ahead, the Italians decided to sit back and hold on to what they had got. It was a big mistake. And manager Marcello Lippi certainly regretted it afterwards.

United responded immediately and began pushing their illustrious visitors back into their own half of the field. Sheringham, calling the tune on his Champions League debut, cleverly set up Solskjaer, but Angelo Peruzzi did well to block his shot, and then United had a goal disallowed when the Norwegian striker deflected Giggs' shot into the net from an offside position.

The crowd could sense that Juventus were on the ropes, and on 37 minutes Old Trafford erupted into a thunderous roar when Sheringham headed in United's equaliser. The lively Giggs crossed from the left, and the England striker nodded the ball down, past Peruzzi and between a host of visiting defenders.

Back on level terms, United were now on top and playing well, and they continued to dictate the game after the interval but without creating as many chances as they would have liked.

There was no denying that Juventus were rattled, and as a result they upped their robust approach, with Uruguayan Paolo Montero a serial offender, but the game plan backfired when their influential midfielder Deschamps received a second yellow card and took an early bath in the 65th minute.

It wasn't long before United took full advantage against ten men. Only 4 minutes after the sending-off, Johnsen flicked a half-cleared corner kick back into the penalty area. Scholes collected the loose ball, fended off substitute Mark Iuliano's attempts to dispossess him, rounded Peruzzi and slotted into the empty net.

The roar that had greeted Sheringham's goal suddenly seemed like a timid yelp in comparison to the baying din that now gripped Old Trafford.

Whereas Juventus had decided to protect their advantage at the start of the game, United went in the opposition direction and went in search of a third goal.

Sheringham twice, Beckham with a screamer and Giggs all came close to increasing United's lead and in the end it was 'Man of the Match' Giggs who wrapped up the victory in the 89th minute with a stunning goal.

Again Sheringham was involved, sliding an inch-perfect pass infield from the left touchline. Giggs raced onto the ball, cleverly jinked his way into the penalty area before letting fly with a fierce shot high into the net past Peruzzi's right hand.

Right at the death, Zidane, who had a quiet game by his standards, struck home a wonderful free kick for Juventus but United held on to record a famous victory – their first over Italian opposition for eighteen years.

United went on to beat Feyenoord 2-1 at home and 3-1 away, and = completed the double over Kocise with another 3-0 victory, but lost the return game against Juventus 1-0 in Turin as they qualified comfortably behind Juvé in Group B. But then it all went wrong as they succumbed to AS Monaco in the quarter-finals, beaten on the away goal rule after a 1-1 draw at Old Trafford, having claimed a 0-0 draw in the away leg.

Juventus progressed to the final, only to lose 1-0 to Real Madrid in Amsterdam.

23

Manchester United 1 Juventus 1
Champions League, Semi-Final, 1st Leg
7 April 1999

Juventus had drawn five of their Group B games to qualify for the knockout stages of the 1998/99 Champions League competition. Not great form really. In fact, they only made it through after beating Rosenborg 2-0 at home in the sixth and final game. Overall, they scored only seven goals while conceding five.

They squeezed past Olympiakos of Greece 3-2 on aggregate in the quarter-finals but, generally speaking, manager Marcello Lippi wasn't at all pleased with the form shown by his midfielders and strikers!

They were well off the pace in Serie A, languishing quite a way behind AC Milan and Lazio, and a lack of goals was certainly causing him some concern.

In contrast, United had finished second in Group D behind Bayern Munich and had ousted Inter Milan 3-1 on aggregate in their quarter-final. They were also on course to win the Premier League title and had already qualified to play Newcastle United in the FA Cup final.

This was the ninth time United and Juventus had met in a major European competition. United had recorded two wins, Juventus five, with one game drawn.

Manchester United (4-4-2): Schmeichel; G. Neville, Berg (Johnsen), Stam, Irwin, Beckham, Scholes, Keane, Giggs, Cole, Yorke (Sheringham).
Juventus (4-4-1-1): Peruzzi; Mirkovic, Montaro (Ferrara), Iuliano, Pessotto, Conte, Deschamps, Davids, Di Livio (Tacchinardi), Zidane, Inzaghi (Esnaider).
Attendance: 54,487

As expected, there was a full house at Old Trafford for this eagerly-awaited encounter.

Dwight Yorke had an early effort for United and soon afterwards Zinedine Zidane chipped over Peter Schmeichel's crossbar. United came again, and from a David Beckham cross Roy Keane returned the ball into the danger zone but Andy Cole headed wide. Then Inzaghi saw his effort saved by Schmeichel.

In the 25th minute Juventus scored to silence the home supporters. Zidane skipped past three United defenders and played in Edgar Davids, who quickly fed in Antonio Conte, who struck a low shot past the diving Schmeichel.

United had a half-chance a few minutes later when a measured cross from Giggs was headed over by Cole. Keane was then yards wide from distance as was Gianluca Pessotto when Juventus counter-attacked.

Early in the second half, with United in attacking mode, substitute Ronny Johnsen headed over, as did Cole, while Scholes also missed the target from an acute pass by Beckham. Angelo Peruzzi was then forced into a fine save to deny Giggs, whose header from Beckham's corner looked goal-bound.

With United on the charge, Keane shot straight at the impressive Peruzzi and, with 15 minutes remaining, Spanish referee Manuel Vega turned down United's appeals for a penalty when Zidane seemed to handle on the edge of the area.

After Schmeichel had saved from the dangerous Conte, United threw bodies forward in a last attempt to grab an equaliser. And they got one, courtesy of Giggs, who found the net from 4 yards after a goalmouth scramble.

Lucky perhaps? But United deserved something on the night.

So onto the return leg in Turin. And what a game it turned out to be. United were without Giggs, Scholes was on the bench and Jesper Blomqvist on the wing. Juventus had Alessandro Birindelli at right-back in place of Zoran Mirkovic.

And after 10 minutes, with 65,497 packed into the Stadio delle Alpi, United looked dead and buried as Juventus took an overall 3-1 lead with two goals by Filippo Inzaghi, the first a stab-in at the far post, his second a deflection off Jaap Stam. Buckling down to the task in hand, Fergie's men hit back strongly. Keane halved the deficit in the 24th minute, and 10 minutes later Yorke headed United level on the night with his twenty-seventh goal of the season – and into the lead overall, courtesy of two vital away goals. With 6 minutes remaining the Turin faithful were stunned when Cole swooped to fire home United's third goal for a 4-3 aggregate victory. What a terrific win, United's first ever on Italian soil. It was, of course, achieved without Giggs, unfortunately, but he was there, cheering on his colleagues as always.

N.B. Keane was yellow-carded in Turin, ruling him out of the final against Bayern Munich.

24

Manchester United 2 Arsenal 1
(After extra time)
FA Cup Semi-Final, Replay
14 April 1999

Following a 0-0 draw after extra time in the first game in front of a full-house Villa Park crowd of 39,217, both managers made changes for the replay.

Dennis Irwin was omitted by Alex Ferguson – largely due, perhaps, to Ray Parlour's Roy Keane impersonation in the first game. Phil Neville was preferred at left-back to partner his brother Gary. And also left out was Ryan Giggs with Jesper Blomqvist taking over.

Arsenal, meanwhile, had midfielder Manu Petit back from suspension; he was brought in to replace Sunday's 'Man of the Match' Nelson Vivas despite his sending-off. In fact this was Arsenal's tenth red card of the season and the twenty-second during Arsene Wenger's reign as Gunners' manager. Marc Overmars, however, was not fully fit and had to settle for a place on the bench.

This was United's twenty-second FA Cup semi-final; for Arsenal it was their twentieth. And lying ahead for the winners of this replay were Newcastle United, who had beaten Tottenham Hotspur 2-0 in the other semi-final.

Arsenal (4-4-2): Seaman; Dixon, Keown, Adams, Winterburn, Vieira, Petit (Bould), Parlour (Kanu), Ljungberg (Overmars), Bergkamp, Anelka.
Manchester United (4-4-2): Schmeichel; G. Neville, Johnsen, Stam, P. Neville, Beckham, Keane, Butt, Solskjaer (Yorke), Sheringham (Scholes), Blomqvist (Giggs).
Attendance: 30,223

The crowd for the replay at Villa Park was 9,000 below capacity when referee David Elleray got proceedings underway. And what a terrific game of football it turned out to be, especially for the neutrals, but it was a horrific one for the Gunners!

United started the better and outplayed Arsenal for most of normal time, missing several good chances. But with the sending off of Roy Keane and the introduction of Marc Overmars in the second half, the balance shifted and in the end the Londoners should have won!

But in the end, two quite stunning individual goals from World Class players swung the game in United's favour.

On another day it could easily have been Dennis Bergkamp and Overmars who took the headlines, but on this occasion it was Ryan Giggs and David Beckham.

United started the sharpest and after just 17 minutes Beckman put his side ahead with a cracking shot. The move started at the back with a Schmeichel clearance. Beckham got a touch, then Solskjaer, and when the ball came back to Beckham, some 22 yards from goal, the wide man let rip with a vicious swirling effort.

England's number one David Seaman, who despite being wrong-footed by the late movement of the ball did well to get back across to his right, was still a foot away from saving the shot.

Bergkamp was clearly up for it, but when he broke through the defence on the right, he could only to poke the ball towards Schmeichel who dived to his right to save.

Then Teddy Sheringham, starting alongside Solskjaer, had a couple of chances. First he shot wide after a smart cut-back from Blomqvist and then headed wide from Beckham's left-wing free kick.

Driven along by Petit and Bergkamp, Arsenal pressed for an equaliser and, when Keane brought Bergkamp down, the Irishman was shown his first yellow card.

Soon afterwards Petit broke into the box, but Schmeichel saved at his near post and the Danish goalkeeper was then relieved to see a shot by Nicolas Anelka fly into the side netting.

United responded and Solskjaer, who beat the offside trap, should have done better when under no pressure and moments later Blomqvist ran clear but his shot was too close to Seaman.

Parlour then set Anelka up in the penalty area but he rushed his shot, which flew over the top.

At this point United introduced Ryan Giggs into the action and immediately he was on the ball … prompting many to ask the question why he had been left out?

United looked dangerous on the break and after, Beckham had shot high and wide, Solskjaer then beat Martin Keown in the chase for a through ball, but Seaman did well to save the striker's low shot.

On 69 minutes, and certainly against the run of play, Arsenal drew level.

Bergkamp, losing his marker, tried a hopeful long shot and was amazed when the ball deflected off of Jaap Stam and flew past Schmeichel. But United came close to regaining the lead within seconds when, following a goalmouth scramble, the ball came to Beckham whose shot went narrowly wide.

After a Bergkamp effort was parried by Schmeichel, Anelka slotted home before seeing an offside flag, with television replays showing that Anelka was offside when Bergkamp delivered his shot.

Seconds later Keane committed another foul, this time on Overmars, and was dismissed, and rightly so.

From that point it became evident how much Keane meant to United. His absence affected the team both in defence and attack, and certainly in midfield as Arsenal started to boss the game. Bergkamp had another effort palmed wide by Schmeichel, and then, right at the end of normal time, Parlour was brought down inside the penalty area by Phil Neville. Bergkamp stepped up to take the resulting spot kick but Schmeichel read it well and, diving to his left, saved the Dutchman's low shot. United had been let off and they knew it.

In extra time it was all Arsenal, and Bergkamp forced another great save from Schmeichel who then did superbly well to block a ricochet off Ronny Johnsson.

Dwight Yorke had come on for United while Wenger introduced Kanu for Parlour and, after Overmars sent a shot swerving wide, Patrick Vieira gave the ball away. His casual pass across the centre line was intercepted by Giggs, but to be fair to the Welshman he had quite a bit left to do! He got past Vieira, Dixon, Keown and Adams, perhaps with a slightly fortunate touch off of Keown in there somewhere, burst into the box on the left, and smashed it over Seaman into the roof of the net. What a goal … it was a real beauty, one of the best ever scored in FA Cup football.

With 10 minutes remaining Arsenal pressed forward and created two good chances. Adams headed a foot wide from Bergkamp's cross before Anelka rushed his shot with the goal in front of him.

United held on, just, to reach their fifteenth FA Cup final and so book a Wembley place against Alan Shearer's Newcastle United on 22 May. But before that showdown against the Geordies, United had to travel to Italy to play the second leg of their Champions League semi-final against Juventus in Turin, and of course they still had seven Premier League games to complete as they went in search of a majestic treble.

25

Manchester United 2 Newcastle United 0
FA Cup Final
22 May 1999

Having won the Premier League title for the fifth time in seven seasons, in-form United were confident of completing the domestic double for the third time, having previously won it in 1994 and 1996. And of course they were in the Champions League final as well.

En route to the FA Cup final United had eliminated Middlesbrough, Liverpool, Fulham, Chelsea and Arsenal, the latter two having finished second and third in the Premier League with Liverpool taking seventh place.

Newcastle, in contrast, had ousted Crystal Palace, Bradford City, Blackburn Rovers, Everton and Tottenham Hotspur, and had ended their Premier League programme in thirteenth position.

David May, Andy Cole, Paul Scholes and Ryan Giggs were included in United's line-up, manager Alex Ferguson choosing to leave a not fully fit Jaap Stam (who was recovering from an Achilles tendons injury), Teddy Sheringham and Dwight Yorke all on the bench.

Newcastle boss Ruud Gullit named Steve Harper in goal in place of Shay Given while omitting defender Warren Barton.

Manchester United (4-4-2): Schmeichel; G. Neville, Johnsen, May, P. Neville, Keane (Sheringham), Beckham, Scholes (Stam), Cole (Yorke), Solskjaer, Giggs.
Newcastle United (4-4-1-1): Harper; Griffin, Domi, Dabizas, Charvet, Solano (Maric), Lee, Hamann (Ferguson), Ketsbaia (Glass), Speed, Shearer.
Attendance: 79,101

Newcastle started well but, after some rather robust tackles, Dietmar Hamann was booked in the 5th minute by Leicestershire referee Peter Jones for a late challenge on Phil Neville.

Newcastle had the first effort at goal when Norberto Solano, receiving Shearer's nod down, hit a shot at Peter Schmeichel who held the ball at the second attempt.

Then, with the game just 9 minutes old, the first significant action saw United's captain Roy Keane receive an injury following a legitimate challenge by Gary Speed.

Keane was replaced by Sheringham and it was the former Spurs striker who gave United the lead with his third touch 2 minutes after coming on. He played a delightful one-two with Paul Scholes before slotting the ball past Steve Harper for the 250th goal of his club career.

The goal, coming as it did, against the run of play, clearly unsettled Newcastle and after Solano's free-kick had whistled over Schmeichel's crossbar Sheringham almost scored a second, but glanced his header wide from Beckham's free-kick.

Despite Newcastle having plenty of possession, they looked vulnerable at the back. Gary Neville's cross was flicked on by Sheringham to Solskjaer who was inches away from converting and then Andy Cole saw his weak lob booted off the line by Laurent Charvet.

Newcastle came again and their Russian striker Temuri Ketsbaia and former Bayern Munich star and future Liverpool and Manchester City midfielder Didier Hamann both came close, the latter seeing his shot well saved by Schmeichel at his near post.

But the threat from Fergie's men remained potent and once again Sheringham came close with a header which went a foot wide of Harper's post.

Gullit sent on Duncan Ferguson at the start of the second half, hoping his aerial power would cause problems in United's defence, but in the 53rd minute a mistake by Greek Nikos Dabizas allowed Ole Gunnar Solskjaer to advance into the penalty area, and his pass to Sheringham was quickly laid off to Scholes who hammered home a second goal.

Newcastle's luck was not in when, a minute after the goal, Ketsbaia's shot struck a post with Schmeichel stranded.

Dwight Yorke replaced the disappointing Cole and immediately United's top scorer should have scored from Giggs's perfect cross, but his header drifted over.

Then a penetrating movement, which contained almost twenty passes, ended when Scholes saw his shot deflected past Harper's post. From the corner, Giggs, who was now tormenting his opponents at will, hit a right-footed volley a yard wide.

It was all United at this stage; Solskjaer scuffed a shot into the hands of Harper and Ronny Johnsen, who had kept Shearer quiet for much of the game, headed Beckham's corner over.

With less than 15 minutes remaining, Scholes was replaced by Jaap Stam, proving that the Dutch defender would be fit for the Champion's League final on Wednesday.

With the game as good as over due to the excellence of United's midfield play and Newcastle's defensive ineptitude, Sheringham came close to scoring his second goal with an acute lob over Harper's crossbar.

A shot from Andy Griffin forced Schmeichel into a last minute save, but a Newcastle goal would have flattered them on an afternoon which belonged to United, who duly completed the double. Now for the treble ... bring on Bayern Munich.

After the final, a delighted Ryan Giggs said: 'We deserved that; we played well and created several good chances. I'm delighted. Now we're ready for Bayern!'

Manchester United 2 Bayern Munich 1
Champions League Final
26 May 1999

United and Bayern Munich had only met twice in competitive matches before this final at Barcelona's Camp Nou. Both had been in the group stage of this season's 1998/99 competition, and had ended in 1-1 and 2-2 draws. For the record, United's only other German opponents in the club's history were Borussia Dortmund, whom they beat three times, suffered two defeats and played out a draw in six European matches.

United had won the European Cup in 1968 whereas Bayern Munich had lifted the coveted trophy on three occasions, doing so in successive seasons 1974–76, being only the third team to achieve such a feat after Real Madrid (1956–60) and Ajax (1971–73). They had also finished runners-up twice in 1982 and 1987. Manchester United had had to wait even longer, their only victory having come in 1968.

On their way to the 1999 final, United started off by defeating LKS Lodz 2-0 on aggregate in the second qualifying round. They then collected ten points out of eighteen in their group, drawing twice with Barcelona, 3-3 each time, whipping Brondby 5-0 and 6-2 and playing out two more draws with Bayern. In the quarter-finals they knocked out Inter Milan (2-0, 1-1) and eliminated another Italian club, Juventus, in the semis (1-1, 3-2; see earlier match report).

Bayern initially overcame FC Obilic (4-0, 1-1), collected 11 points in their group with two wins over Barcelona (1-0, 2-1), victory over Brondby (2-0) and draws against United (twice), while losing away to Brondby. In the last eight they ousted FC Kaiserslautern (2-0, 4-0) before accounting for Dynamo Kiev in the semis (1-0, 3-3).

United manager Alex Ferguson selected Jaap Stam at the heart of the defence but Roy Keane (suspended) and Paul Scholes were both out. Bayern, basically at full strength, were favourites to win the star prize. Ryan Giggs, however, said before the game, 'We are up for this. We have been playing well and having already won the Premier League title and the FA Cup, we can now achieve something special by lifting the Champions League trophy and complete a unique treble.'

Bayern Munich (1-4-2-3): Kahn; Matthäus, Babbel, Linke, Kuffour, Tarnat, Effenberg, Jeremies, Basler (Salihamidzic), Jancker, Zickler (Scholl).
Manchester United (4-4-2): Schmeichel; G. Neville, Johnsen, Stam, Irwin, Giggs, Beckham, Butt, Blomqvist (Sheringham), Yorke, Cole (Solskjaer).
Attendance: 90,245

6 minutes into the match, United defender Ronny Johnsen fouled Bayern striker Carsten Jancker just outside the area. Mario Basler took the free-kick and scored!

United were stunned and for a while struggled to make an impression on the German defence despite David Beckham's tireless running. It was evident they were badly missing influential midfielders Scholes and Keane as the Bayern back line remained strong and well organised, Andy Cole did find space but his close-range effort was immediately closed down by three defenders.

With Bayern looking increasingly more dangerous on the counter-attack, Jancker repeatedly tested the United back four with a number of clever runs, some of which were flagged offside.

Cole once again had a chance but keeper Oliver Kahn raced out of his goal to punch the ball to safety. At the other end, Mario Basler came close with another free kick before Alexander Zickler fired wide from the edge of the box. As half-time approached, Giggs, playing out of position on the right, sent a weak header towards Kahn from a Cole cross, but that was as close as they were to come to a goal in the first half.

Bayern started the second half in a more positive mood with Jancker forcing a smart save from Schmeichel in the 46th minute.

Workaholic Basler was proving to be Bayern's most dangerous player, first firing in a 30-yard shot and then setting up a header for Markus Babbel, who thankfully, from United's point of view, missed the ball entirely.

United at last put together a worthy attack and, from Giggs' tempting cross, Jesper Blomqvist could only knock the ball over the bar after a desperate stretch.

Another chance for Basler prompted Alex Ferguson to bring on striker Teddy Sheringham in the 67th minute. Bayern manager Ottmar Hitzfeld responded with a substitution of his own, bringing on Mehmet Scholl, who immediately set up Stefan Effenberg for a long-range shot which fizzed wide. Then Schmeichel kept United in the game by tipping another Effenberg effort over the bar after 75 minutes.

With United on the back foot, Scholl almost scored from a delicate 20-yard chip after a fine run from Basler, but the ball came back off the post and into the arms of a relieved Schmeichel.

With the game seemingly drifting away from United, Fergie introduced striker Ole Gunnar Solskjaer with 10 minutes remaining. And immediately the Norwegian forced Kahn into a diving save with a header. It was the closest United had come to scoring all game.

Seconds later, Bayern almost secured victory when Jancker's overhead kick came back into play off the crossbar. With 5 minutes remaining, United's two substitutes forced Kahn into diving saves, Sheringham with a volley and a header from Solskjaer.

Then, as Italian referee Pierluigi Collina looked at his watch, United won a corner just as the fourth official indicated 3 minutes of injury time.

With so little time left for an equaliser, Schmeichel ventured upfield. Beckham's flighted corner drifted just over the keeper's head, but Yorke was there to get the ball back into the crowded area. And when Thorsten Fink failed to clear his lines, the ball fell at the feet of Giggs on the edge of the box. His right-footed snap shot lacked pace but the ball went straight to Sheringham, whose right-footed shot flew into the bottom corner of Kahn's net. No one could believe it; United had equalised at the death. The goal was officially timed at 90:36.

Having been behind for most of the match, it seemed as if United had forced extra time. But amazingly, just 30 seconds after that goal, United forced another corner.

This time Schmeichel, having been instructed to remain in his penalty area, watched Beckham's measured flag-kick find the head of Sheringham, who nodded the ball down across the face of goal. Solskjaer reacted fastest, stuck out a foot and poked the ball into the roof of the Bayern net. What a finish. United were in front, totally unexpected, and this stunning second goal was timed at 92:17.

Solskjaer celebrated by sliding on his knees, mimicking Basler's earlier celebration, before being mobbed by his delighted colleagues, substitutes and even the coaching staff while Schmeichel, 100 yards away, cart-wheeled with glee. What joy!

The game restarted, but many of the Bayern players were overwhelmed with despair, virtually unable to continue, and referee Collina had to step in to ensure they completed the match.

The Bayern players were distraught, having lost a game they thought they had won!

In fact, several celebratory flares had already been ignited by their fans moments before United equalised and the German club's ribbons had already been secured to the trophy itself in preparation for the presentation ceremony.

United comfortably held out and at the final whistle Samuel Kuffour broke down in tears, beating the turf in despair. Even the giant Carsten Jancker collapsed in anguish, as did Effenberg and Scholl.

Bayern's captain Matthäus was also tearful on the touchline, having lost the 1987 final in similar circumstances to two late FC Porto goals. The trophy was duly presented to United's skipper Peter Schmeichel – who had just completed his final match for the club – and manager Alex Ferguson, and they raised the silver pot together as the rest of the players and staff joined in the celebrations. What a terrific night it turned out to be in Spain.

After everything had calmed down, to a certain degree, an emotional Giggs said: 'I told you so; we didn't play well but we knew we would finish the stronger and so it proved.'

27

Manchester United 4 West Ham United 2
Premier League
18 December 1999

Three days before this Premier League game at Upton Park, West Ham had beaten Aston Villa on penalties to reach the semi-finals of the League Cup. But just forty-eight hours later, it emerged that the London club had selected a cup-tied player, Manny Omoyinmi, and could be thrown out of the competition.

Omoyinmi had only played the last 7 minutes of extra time after coming off the bench and did not take a spot kick, but none of that mattered: West Ham were in trouble. Villa insisted they should be thrown out, but eventually it was agreed that a replay should take place at Upton Park in January.

United, meanwhile, had been in good form and had won five of their previous six League games, hammering Everton 5-1 in the process.

Manager Alex Ferguson made a handful of changes from the team that had seen off the Merseysiders, bringing in Raimond Van der Gouw in goal (for Mark Bosnich), David Beckham on the right side of midfield and Dwight Yorke in attack. And Ryan Giggs, who had been outstanding over a six-week period, was looking forward to the match, saying, 'We always do well against West Ham, and hopefully we can gain another win, having beaten them 4-1 at Old Trafford earlier in the year.'

West Ham United (4-4-2): Hislop; Sinclair, Ferdinand, Ruddock, Minto, Lampard, Lomas, Fox, Keller, Di Canio, Wanchope.
Manchester United (4-4-2): Van der Gouw; G. Neville, Stam, Silvestre, Irwin (P. Neville) Beckham (Butt), Scholes, Keane, Giggs, Yorke, Sheringham.
Attendance: 26,037

Everyone inside Upton Park was in a state of shock following the news of their League Cup fiasco.

The mood was certainly flat and United wasted no time twisting the knife. After a couple of decent attacks, future Old Trafford defender Rio Ferdinand ending one of them with a timely interception, they took the lead on 10 minutes when an unmarked Dwight Yorke headed home David Beckham's inch-perfect cross.

3 minutes later Yorke turned provider, crossing for Giggs to flick the ball cleverly past goalkeeper Shaka Hislop for United's second. And with only 19 minutes played, and with the Hammers' defence seemingly all at sea, Giggs smashed home a terrific volley from fully 25 yards into the bottom-left corner to make it three-nil.

At this point, West Ham – undefeated in four League games and lying ninth in the table – were simply 'all over the place', as one pundit commented. And their disgruntled manager Harry Redknapp started to prowl the touchline, scratching his head and looking totally frustrated.

Yet the Londoners managed to drag themselves back into the match, totally against the run of play it must be said.

In the 25th minute, former Lazio, Napoli, Juventus, AC Milan and Celtic star Paolo Di Canio had enough space to try his luck with a scissor-kick. And the attempt came off, as the ball skimmed under Van der Gouw to give the home side a lifeline. But surely that was just a minor inconvenience for United, wasn't it?

It was nothing of the sort. Urged on by their fans, the Hammers, with Frank Lampard in the thick of the action, pressed United back and only some stern defending by Jaap Stam and Frenchman Mikael Silvestre, and a fine save by Van der Gouw, prevented further goals.

7 minutes into the second half, industrious French midfielder Marc Keller slipped a neat pass through to the alert Di Canio, who drew Van der Gouw out of position, jinked to the goalkeeper's left and simply tapped the ball into the empty net, to the considerable delight of the BBC's Barry Davies!

3-2, game on. United were fearing the worst as the revitalised Hammers went in search of an equaliser. They were not immune to relinquishing healthy leads at Upton Park, as one reporter recalled: 'In December 1996, they were 2-0 up with 12 minutes left but drew 2-2, Julian Dicks almost taking Peter Schmeichel's head off with the equalising penalty in a match that featured an exquisite Beckham chip'.

But back to this encounter in 1999. United were rocking and West Ham, inspired by their Italian international Di Canio, who was in the form of his life, were on top and looking strong.

Shortly after his second goal, Di Canio charged through United's defence again, his hat-trick goal and West Ham's equaliser seemingly an inevitability.

He dropped a shoulder as he attempted to trick Van der Gouw for a second time, but on this occasion the Dutchman stood firm, not over-committing himself in anyway.

This wasn't in the script, they said, and Di Canio, stuttering in his stride, tried to chip the ball over United's keeper but it barely left the ground and Van der Gouw saved easily.

As a result, United – who could easily have been pegged back – exacted swift and brutal punishment.

In the 62nd minute, Giggs, taking a pass in his stride, burst past former Manchester City player Steve Lomas on the left and, as Sheringham distracted Ferdinand, he crossed perfectly for Yorke to guide home his second goal of the match and his tenth of the season to re-establish United's two-goal advantage.

It was effectively game over for the home side. United came close to scoring twice more through Giggs and substitute Nicky Butt, and with West Ham offering little at this stage, Fergie's men held on fairly comfortably to register a deserved win and so move into top spot in the table ahead of Leeds United. But it had been some game.

United went on to complete the double over the Hammers, whipping them 7-1 in the return fixture at Old Trafford on April Fool's Day – without Ryan Giggs I might add!

And for the record, West Ham lost 3-1 to Aston Villa in their 'replayed' League Cup tie.

28

Manchester United 1 Bayern Munich 2
(United lost 1-3 on aggregate)
Champions League, Quarter-Final, 2nd Leg
18 April 2001

Having lost the first leg of their Champions League quarter-final encounter with title-holders Bayern Munich by a goal to nil at Old Trafford a fortnight earlier, United knew that the return clash would be their biggest test of the season.

Well on course for their seventh Premier League title, they travelled to Germany on the back of successive home wins over Charlton Athletic and Coventry City, but manager Alex Ferguson was a little concerned about the number of goals his defence had been conceding ... six in their last four competitive matches.

Bayern, meanwhile, were battling it out for the Bundesliga title with FC Schalke and Borussia Dortmund. They were also in good form and were confident of progressing into the last four.

This fixture was a repeat of the 1999 final which United won 2-1, and everyone associated with Bayern Munich wanted revenge! As one punter said to a United supporter: 'You've won three wars already, we will win this one!'

David Beckham was out of the United side, but Jaap Stam was named at the heart of the defence while Dwight Yorke and Andy Cole were named as the two main strikers, with Ryan Giggs assisting whenever possible.

As for Bayern, Frenchman Bixente Lizarazu was replaced by Michael Tarnat and the Bosnian international Hasan Salihamidzic by Willy Sagnol.

Bayern Munich (4-4-2): Kahn; Kuffour, Andersson, Linke, Sagnol, Tarnat, Jeremies, Effenberg, Scholl, Jancker (Zickler), Elber (Santa Cruz).
Manchester United (4-4-2): Barthez; G. Neville, Brown, Stam, Silvestre, Scholes, Keane, Butt (Solskjaer), Giggs, Yorke (Sheringham), Cole.
Attendance: 59,892

Referee Victor Pereira of Portugal set the game underway inside a packed Allianz Arena and straightaway Bayern pressed forward. It looked to be a tame start, but then, out of nothing, Tarnat ran clear down the left and, from his cross, the Brazilian Giovane Elber headed the hosts into the lead. It was disastrous start for United, two down on aggregate with it all to do.

Shortly afterwards Jancker cracked a shot against Fabian Barthez's crossbar from 10 yards and, with United's defence all at sea, the same player was stopped in his tracks by Mikael Silvestre's challenge ... Yorke had a sniff of a chance on 14 minutes before United won their first corner, which came to nothing. And then it was that man Jancker who almost scored again, but missed the target.

After Giggs had fired in United's first real effort on goal, the Welshman was denied an opening by the foot of Jeremies.

It was end-to-end stuff and after Cole had prodded a shot wide from 6 yards, the striker then saw another effort cleared off the line. United were looking good as Paul Scholes blasted his volley wide of the post.

But then on 40 minutes, Jeremies out on the right found Elber inside the penalty area with a superb cross. The ball was knocked on to substitute Zickler who in turn flicked it to Scholl who beat Barthez at the far post. A wonderful move.

Bayern pulled ten men behind the ball whenever possible and, on the stroke of half-time, a Giggs corner was put onto the roof of the net by Cole.

After a bright start to the second half, United pulled a goal back on 49 minutes. Scholes fed Giggs who, controlling the ball, coolly lobbed it over Kahn from 15 yards ... an excellent piece of work.

United had come out fighting but Bayern were still dangerous on the break and Stam had to check Zickler just outside the area, but Andersson blasted the free kick into the wall. On the hour mark, Kahn saved a 20-yard volley from Giggs who was now causing a few problems down Bayern's left.

Sheringham came on for Yorke as United continued to look dangerous and, after one worthy attack, strong appeals for a penalty were brushed aside as Kuffour appeared to fall into the back of Cole 3 yards out.

Needing a goal to win, Fergie sent on Ole Gunnar Solskjaer with 12 minutes remaining but it was Bayern who almost scored again, Zickler firing over from Effenberg's pass.

Sheringham then fired over a blinding cross which Cole failed to convert; Scholes powered in a drive from 20 yards out which was tuned over by Kahn and Sheringham put a good chance wide.

As Silvestre chased back, so Zickler went down – no penalty and then Chadwick beat three players but chose to a pass to Keane when a crack at goal looked the better option

With time running out, Sheringham fired into the ground and, from Giggs' late corner, Cole and Yorke were shut out by Linke and Sagnol.

So, after a terrific game of football, it was Bayern who moved into the semi-finals, where they met and beat Real Madrid before going on to defeat Valencia 5-4 in the final in Milan.

After losing to Bayern, Giggs was somewhat downbeat when he said: 'We were perhaps the better side on the night. They defended well and for that reason, they won the game. I'm obviously disappointed, so too are the rest of the lads but we'll bounce back as usual'.

29

Bayer 04 Leverkusen 1 Manchester United 1
(aggregate score 3-3;
United lost on away goal rule)
Champions League, Semi-Final, 2nd Leg
30 April 2002

The question everyone seemed to be asking was how would United approach the return leg of this semi-final, having been held to a 2-2 draw by Leverkusen in the first game at Old Trafford. They knew they had to try and keep a clean sheet and score at least one goal! It was not going to be easy.

Manager Alex Ferguson admitted that if Leverkusen found the net, especially early on, it would mean that United would have a much tougher task on their hands. 'We would have a mountain to climb,' he said.

Fergie decided to select a rather defensive line-up, but he did name two top-class strikers on the bench, saying, 'I know what lies ahead and what we have to do on the pitch. We'll have to be at our best; we need to play well and hope they have an off day. We can do it, but it will be hard.'

Going into this game in Germany, United had lost only once in twelve competitive games – a 1-0 home Premier League defeat by Middlesbrough. They were no longer in the title race – this was now between Arsenal and Liverpool and it was the Gunners who went on to claim the prize with a 1-0 victory at Old Trafford on 8 May as United were left without a trophy for the first time in thirteen seasons.

On their way to the semi-finals, United had finished second in Group G behind Deportivo La Coruna and then topped Group A in the second group stage before beating La Coruna (5-2 on aggregate) in the quarter-finals.

Leverkusen, who were fighting it out with Borussia Dortmund at the top of the German Bundesliga, had progressed via Group F (after beating Barcelona 2-1) and as Stage Group D winners before knocking out Liverpool 4-3 on aggregate in the quarter-finals.

Bayer 04 Leverkusen (4-4-1-1): Butt; Zivkovic, Nowotny (Sebescen), Lucio, Placente, Schneider, Ballack, Ramelow, Ze Roberto, Basturk (Vranjes), Neuville.

Manchester United (4-4-1-1): Barthez; Brown (Forlan), Blanc, Johnsen (Irwin), Silvestre, Scholes, Keane, Butt (Solskjaer), Giggs, Veron, van Nistelrooy.

Attendance: 22,488

Referee Milton Nielsen from Denmark got the game underway in front of a full house inside the Bay Arena.

Wes Brown was selected at right-back with fit-again Ronny Johnsen named as Laurent Blanc's partner at the heart of the defence. Alex Ferguson also chose to use Ruud van Nistelrooy as a lone striker, hopefully supported by Juan Sebastian Veron, with Paul Scholes, Roy Keane, Nicky Butt and Ryan Giggs there to assist as well, with the latter being asked to attack with speed down the left.

Leverkusen, approaching the game in a cautious manner, lost their central defender Jens Nowotny with a knee injury as early as the 9th minute, following a tussle with van Nistelrooy, but on 12 minutes they almost scored. Bernt Schneider gathered an inside pass from Diego Placente, spotted Fabien Barthez off his line, and produced a delightful chip which rebounded off the post. That was a close call. 4 minutes later, from Giggs's corner, Johnsen's downward header was cleared off the line by the active Placente.

United were looking strong and deservedly took the lead in the 28th minute. Keane picked up a pass from Veron, accepted a return ball from van Nistelrooy, and, running on the blind side of the Leverkusen defence, he beat Hans-Jörg Butt with a low drive from a narrow angle. Now with the initiative, United pressed hard and, after a couple of quick raids, Yildiray Basturk just managed to deflect Veron's angled drive over the bar.

Twice Leverkusen had come back at Old Trafford to level the scores and in the return leg they did so again when Oliver Neuville, United's nemesis in the first match, found the net in stoppage-time at the end of the first half ... soon after he had smashed a shot against United's crossbar.

United had looked in control of the game and, in fact, were threatening to increase their lead. But some slack marking proved fatal. And manager Fergie wasn't at all happy! The second half was rather scrappy although both teams created chances, Leverkusen having the best opportunities to take the lead, but Barthez saved well from Ze Roberto and Michael Ballack.

In fact, with barely 3 minutes remaining, United came close, mightily close, to winning the tie. Uruguayan international Diego Forlan, who had followed Ole Gunnar Solskjaer off the bench as Fergie filled his team with strikers, produced a rocket of a shot which beat Butt in the Leverkusen goal only to be headed off the line by 'Man of the Match' Placente. Leverkusen buckled down held on for a draw and so gain an overall victory courtesy of their two away goals scored at Old Trafford.

Part of United's problem on the night lay in the fact that, with Leverkusen holding a strong advantage with those two away goals, they had to try to win the game while guarding against going hell for leather for a victory.

United, it must be said, had the better of the second half in terms of possession, but they were unable to carve out a clear-cut chance until late on.

So sadly, United's and Ryan Giggs' dreams of winning a second Champions League were extinguished in Germany. It was the third time a German side had reached the Champions League final at Hampden Park, but it would not be a joyous occasion in Scotland in mid-May. Spanish giants Real Madrid, who knocked out arch-rivals Barcelona in the other semi-final, won 2-1 to lift the trophy for the third time in five years.

30

Manchester United 6 West Ham United 0
FA Cup 4th Round
25 January 2003

Having knocked out Portsmouth 4-1 in the opening round, and with four successive Premier League victories behind him, plus the fact they had also qualified for the League Cup final after beating Blackburn Rovers over two legs in the semis, United were beaming in confidence ahead of this encounter with the Hammers, who were in deep, deep trouble at the foot of the table and winless in fourteen League games.

Sir Alex Ferguson named an unchanged team for the third game in a row while his counterpart, Glenn Roeder, was missing at least three key players. But he did have future United player Michael Carrick available and named ex-Reds goalkeeper Raimond van der Gouw on the subs bench.

Manchester United (4-4-1-1): Barthez, G. Neville, Ferdinand, O'Shea, P. Neville, Beckham (Solskjaer), Veron (Butt), Keane, Giggs, Scholes (Forlan), van Nistelrooy.
West Ham United (4-4-2): James; Lomas, Breen (Dailly), Pearce, Minto, Bowyer, Cisse (Garcia), Carrick, Sinclair (Johnson), Defoe, Cole.
Attendance: 67,181

United, with Ryan Giggs, Ruud van Nistelrooy and David Beckham quite outstanding, turned on the style to charge into the fifth round of the FA Cup while at the same time rubbing salt into West Ham's gaping Premier League wounds.

The Hammers were desperately in need of a good performance to take their minds off their awful Premier Legaue form, but they were completely outplayed at Old Trafford as United romped to a comfortable victory.

Giggs and van Nistelrooy both struck twice in an embarrassingly one-sided game, with defender Phil Neville and substitute Ole Gunnar Solskjaer also joining the goal scoring spree as an inept West Ham hardly mustered a worthwhile attack. It took Fergie's side just 8 minutes to break through the fragile-looking Hammers defence.

Dutch striker van Nistelrooy, watching and waiting, easily shrugged off a weak challenge from Gary Breen to reach David Beckham's pass and tee up Paul Scholes. His shot was booted off the line by the retreating Ian Pearce but the ball fell kindly to Giggs, who calmly stroked it home, right-footed through a crowd of players on the line.

After continuous pressure, several shots and crosses, United deservedly doubled their lead in the 29th minute when Giggs, who incidentally had scored only once in his previous twenty-five games, gleefully bagged his second of the game.

The Argentine midfielder Sebastian Juan Veron teed up the winger on the edge of the Hammers' penalty area and the Welshman's first-time shot looped off Gary Breen and over the helpless David James, who was static between the posts.

Although this was an all-Premier League cup tie, on the balance of play it seemed as if it was giants against lower division minnows, so badly were West Ham playing! United continued to drive forward and goalkeeper James had to be at his agile best to keep out a curling right-foot shot from Beckham.

Then the Hammers' over-worked keeper needed a post to come to his rescue 10 minutes before half-time when a superb sequence of passes ended with van Nistelrooy setting up Scholes for a shot against the woodwork.

Scholes, who had complained of feeling unwell towards the interval, was replaced for the second half by striker Diego Forlan who was straight into the action, forcing Breen into conceding a corner.

West Ham simply had nowhere to go, and with United coming at them like a swarm of bees, and with Giggs in magical form, the already rumbling stomachs of their defenders turned even more in the 49th minute.

The hard-to-mark van Nistelrooy twisted and turned on the edge of the box and, with three West Ham defenders bumping into each other, the striker took full advantage of the carnage to majestically clip a shot past James with the outside of his right boot.

50 seconds later, West Ham conceded again as United's full-back Phil Neville played a one-two with Forlan, brushed aside a flimsy challenge and skipped clear to plant a left-foot shot over James to double his goal tally for the season.

With van Nistelrooy enjoying so much space, it was he who duly added a fifth goal with half an hour still to play. After a weak clearance by James, Beckham played a pass through the legs of the hapless Pearce and, as the centre of Hammers' defence disappeared once more, the Dutchman pounced to lash home his second goal of the game.

The inspired van Nistelrooy then turned provider for United's sixth goal 20 minutes from time. Turning smartly, he played a splendid ball through for substitute Ole Gunnar Solskjaer who ran forward before drilling a low right-foot shot past the frustrated James.

West Ham may well have had a late penalty when Gary Neville clipped the ankles of Joe Cole, but referee Steve Bennett waved play on.

Michael Carrick was hardly involved in midfield as Messrs Beckham, Butt, Giggs and co. ran the show from start to finish.

BBC correspondent Mike Ingham said, 'West Ham were abysmal' and United boss Alex Ferguson admitted, 'It was a good performance by us but the opposition was poor.'

31

Manchester United 3 Juventus 0
Champions League, Second Stage, Group D
25 February 2003

Having beaten Juventus 2-1 at Old Trafford six days earlier, United travelled to Italy on a high. Unbeaten since Boxing Day and lying second in the Premier League table (behind Arsenal), they had a League Cup final encounter against Liverpool in a week's time.

United had already scored five goals against FC Zalaegerszeg from Bosnia and Herzegovina in their initial two-legged qualify tie and sixteen in Group F to reach the second stage of the competition.

In the first phase, Juventus had eased through Group F with four wins out of six, and were on course to win the Serie A title for the twenty-seventh time.

Manager Sir Alex Ferguson named both Ryan Giggs and Ruud van Nistelrooy on the bench, choosing Diego Forlan and Ole Gunnar Solskjaer up front with a forceful-looking midfield behind them, although he had lost Mikael Silvestre through injury, slotting Roy Keane into the back division.

Juventus had one of the best midfielders in Europe (at that time), Pavel Nedved, as part of their attack while Gianluigi Buffon was between the posts, having missed the first game.

Juventus (4-4-2): Buffon; Thuram, Zambrotta (Pessotto), Camoranesi, Ferrara, Montero, Conte (Tudor), Nedved, Trezeguet, Di Vaio (Salas), Davids.
Manchester United (4-4-2): Barthez; G. Neville, Keane, Ferdinand, O'Shea (Pugh), P. Neville, Beckham, Butt, Veron, Solskjaer, Forlan (Gibbs, then van Nistelrooy).
Attendance: 59,111

There was a tremendous atmosphere inside the Stadio Delle Alpi as German referee Markus Merk got the game underway, and it was Nedved who put the first effort miles wide – nearer the corner flag than the goal.

And when Juventus attacked again, a crucial touch from Keane deflected a dangerous pass from Nedved. Almost immediately, Forlan was carried off on a stretcher and replaced by Giggs, and the Welshman was soon in action, attempting to thread the ball through to Nicky Butt but, the alert Buffon cleared up.

Di Vaio then beat Keane for pace but as he shot, the Irishman got back to concede a 14th minute corner from which Ciro Ferrara rattled Barthez's crossbar with a header.

United charged straight downfield. The ball found its way through to Beckham who picked out Solskjaer with a terrific cross-field pass. The striker, in turn, fed Veron on the right wing and after rounding Zambrotta (who slipped), the Argentine crossed to Giggs who, finding space, cleverly rolled the ball home past Buffon. A great goal.

A horrifically bad chested back-pass from Zambrotta almost let in Solskjaer for a second goal but bravery from Buffon averted the danger.

Next, Trezeguet went over after a challenge from O'Shea but all penalty shouts fell on deaf ears. I have seen plenty given for similar challenges.

Keane was having a blinder and twice in as many minutes he cleared his lines, although he did, it seemed, handle inside the penalty area, but none of the Juventus players saw it. The crowd did, though.

In the 32nd minute, Trezeguet rattled United's crossbar, but it was in truth a terrible miss by the Frenchman, who was allowed a free header from Camoranesi's cross.

Juventus were pulling the strings and could easily have scored four goals, but they had squandered chance after chance, although Butt missed a sitter when one-on-one with Buffon. He lifted the ball over the keeper but saw it come back off the crossbar.

In the 40th minute United went two up, Giggs scoring with a near replica of the goal he netted in the 1999 FA Cup semi-final replay win over Arsenal.

Perhaps it wasn't quite as good, but it was certainly a bit special. Embarking on a weaving run, he glided past four or five static Juventus players before sending the ball low past Buffon's right hand.

After scoring twice, and having given the Juventus defence plenty to think about, the unfortunate Giggs had come off with a niggling injury, replaced by van Nistelrooy.

After Trezeguet missed the target again, Salas flicked a header over while, at the other end of the field, Solskjaer was denied by a great save from Buffon.

Soon after Mancunian Danny Pugh, aged twenty, had come on for O'Shea, United scored a third goal in the 61st minute through van Nistelrooy who found himself completely unmarked to slot home. Dreadful defending.

With United on a roll, Gary Neville saw his chip bounce off the crossbar and a solid tackle by Pugh stopped Mauro Camoranesi in his tracks. Juventus were being made to look like ham-fisted amateurs in front of their own fans. United were loving it!

Juventus had completely given up the ghost. Only midfielder Conte was showing any interest and although Camoranesi fired in a long-range effort, Veron headed over at the other end. Davids then shot wide, Nedved was block-tackled by Keane and after that United simply strolled through to victory.

A delighted Giggs said after the game, 'To score a goal like my second against Juventus or indeed, against any Italian team, was very special for me. I hadn't been playing well for a few weeks. In fact, it hadn't been one of my best seasons up to that point.'

Unfortunately, United lost to Real Madrid in the quarter-finals (see report); Juventus reached the final but lost 3-2 on penalties to AC Milan.

32

Liverpool 2 Manchester United 0
League Cup Final
2 March 2003

En route to the final, United had ousted Leicester City 2-0, Burnley 2-0, Chelsea 1-0 and Blackburn Rovers 4-2 over two legs in the semi-final.

Liverpool had knocked out Southampton 3-1, Ipswich Town 5-4 on penalties (after a 2-2 draw), Aston Villa 4-3 and Sheffield United 3-2 on aggregate in the two-legged semi-final.

Alex Ferguson, in a confident mood, was pleased to have Ryan Giggs, Paul Scholes and Wes Brown all fit to take their places, while Liverpool boss Gerard Houllier also had a full squad to choose from.

United were unbeaten in eight Premier League games going into the final. Liverpool on the other hand had only won two of their previous sixteen League games, a run which included a 2-1 home defeat by United. Both clubs had been knocked out of the FA Cup. Liverpool had been eliminated from the Champions League but were still in the UEFA Cup, while United were set to face Real Madrid in the quarter-finals of the Champions League.

It was certainly a hectic period for both clubs and for the record books, when the season came to a close, the combined total of competitive matches played by United and Liverpool in 2003/04 stood at 123. United competed in sixty-four of them with Ryan Giggs taking part in fifty-nine.

Liverpool (4-4-2): Dudek; Carragher, Henchoz, Hyypia, Riise, Diouf (Biscan), Hamann, Gerrard, Murphy, Owen, Heskey (Baros, then Smicer).
Manchester United (4-5-1): Barthez, G. Neville, Brown (Solskjaer), Ferdinand, Silvestre, Beckham, Keane, Veron, Scholes, Giggs, van Nistelrooy.
Attendance: 74,390

Liverpool perhaps deserved to win on the day, but it was their goalkeeper Jerzy Dudek who was the star of the show. He was quite superb between the posts, keeping United at bay with some excellent saves.

Dudek had been at fault earlier in the season when he presented Uruguayan striker Diego Forlan with a goal in United's Premier League win at Anfield, but he exorcised his demons in tremendous style, proving the cornerstone of Liverpool's win in front of a near full house at Cardiff's Millennium Stadium.

The opening stages of this, the forty-third League Cup final (the first was in 1961), were, in truth, action-free as both sides eyed each other up.

It wasn't until the 21st minute that the first chance was created and it was United who almost broke the deadlock. Scholes released Giggs, and his cross found Dutch striker Ruud van Nistelrooy whose precise flick drifted only inches wide of Dudek's far post.

After some purposeful attacks by United, and a prolonged period of Liverpool pressure which saw future United striker Michael Owen, after a darting run, thwarted by a sprawling block by French goalkeeper Fabien Barthez, the Merseysiders took the lead 6 minutes before the interval, at a time when United were perhaps on top.

The breakthrough goal, however, had a touch of good fortune attached to it. The impressive Steven Gerrard, taking advantage of David Beckham's failure to close him down, collected John Arne Riise's pass and powered in a shot from fully 25 yards. With Barthez right behind it, the ball suddenly took a wicked deflection off Beckham and looped over the United keeper and into the unguarded net.

Liverpool then had an astonishing escape on the stroke of half-time when Dudek first blocked a strong shot from Juan Sebastian Veron. The rebound fell to the feet of Scholes, whose well-guided effort was turned over the top by defender Stephane Henchoz from virtually under the crossbar.

United, as they had to do, pushed more men forward from the start of the second-half. Giggs, Beckham and Scholes all tried their luck. Indeed, Liverpool were grateful for Dudek's instinctive reaction save to deny van Nistelrooy on the hour mark. Meanwhile, Dorset referee Paul Durkin waved aside dubious penalty claims from both sides.

At this juncture, Houllier brought on striker Milan Baros as the tightly contested game began to open up a lot more. And it was Barthez who kept United alive, saving a brilliant close-range effort from Gerrard after Baros had broken clear on the counter attack.

Suddenly the game was alive, and with the crowd roaring United almost equalised, but 'Man of the Match' Dudek once again denied the adventurous Scholes. Giggs and Keane also put in efforts and as United drove forward. And after Dudek had saved his side yet again, this time from van Nistelrooy, and with Liverpool living on a knife edge, it was suddenly game over for United in the 86th minute.

German Dietmar Hamann released Owen. The striker raced on, unchallenged, to beat Barthez with a clinical finish. United were beaten.

After a dogged, evenly balanced contest, Liverpool had four players who produced something special when it mattered most ... Dudek, Gerrard, Henchoz and ace marksman Owen. For United, Beckham, Scholes, van Nistelrooy and Giggs played their part but in the end disappointed United boss, Sir Alex simply saying, 'The deciding factor was Liverpool's goalkeeper Jerzy Dudek – he was magnificent.'

And Giggs agreed: 'He was outstanding. All credit to Liverpool, they played well, but so did we. But there could be only one winner and it wasn't us'.

33

Manchester United 6 Newcastle United 2
Premier League
12 April 2003

With just six games remaining, the race for the Premier League title was hotting up nicely. United, who were on a twelve-match unbeaten run in the championship, had whipped Fulham 3-0 and Liverpool 4-0 in their two previous home games and were in pretty good form. Manager Alex Ferguson was happy that at this stage of the season very few players were unavailable. Indeed, with Real Madrid expected to offer around £40 million for David Beckham, he chose to leave his star man out of his starting line-up against Newcastle.

Earlier in the season when United were lying fifth in the top division, they beat Newcastle (eighth) 5-3 at Old Trafford, Ruud van Nistelrooy scoring a hat-trick in 15 minutes either side of half-time.

'Fergie' and his troops were hoping for a repeat performance (goal-wise) and of course another victory which would enhance their title ambitions.

Newcastle United (4-3-1-2): Given, Hughes, Bramble, Woodgate, Bernard, Solano (Ameobi), Dyer, Jenas, Robert (Viana), Shearer, Bellamy, Viana (Lua-Lua).
Manchester United (4-4-2): Barthez, O'Shea (G. Neville), Ferdinand, Brown (Blanc), Silvestre, Keane, Butt, Scholes, Giggs (Forlan), Solskjaer, van Nistelrooy.
Attendance: 52,164

United went out and produced a ruthless performance at St James' Park to move three points clear of Arsenal at the top of the Premier League table while at the same time stretching their lead over third-placed Newcastle, who in January had actually held pole position.

This resounding victory over Sir Bobby Robson's side on Tyneside set the scene perfectly for the huge championship showdown at Highbury between the Gunners and in-form United in four days' time which in effect was a mightily important and, indeed, crucial six-pointer.

To add to Arsenal's anxiety, United's sensational scoring spree was a significant factor, putting a severe dent in the Gunners' goal difference advantage.

Only a late goal from Newcastle's Shola Ameobi kept Arsenal in front on that score, but it was a minor blot on a night when United were supreme in every department.

United surprisingly allowed Newcastle the luxury of an early lead through Jermaine Jenas before turning on the style to completely destroy the Toons.

The rampant Reds struck four times before the interval through Ole Gunnar Solskjaer (32 minutes), a Paul Scholes double (34 and 38) and Ryan Giggs (44).

Scholes, who was brilliant throughout, completed his hat-trick in the 52nd minute before Ruud van Nistelrooy provided the final flourish from the penalty spot just before the hour mark. And during the last half hour, United created at least another six changes as he ran rings round a bemused Newcastle defence. It was a good job that goalkeeper Shay Given was in pretty good form or the victory margin may well have been ten and not four!

This victory by United was the perfect response to their 3-1 Champions League defeat at the hands of Real Madrid a few days earlier – and, of course, it was the ideal preparation for the crunch encounter with Arsenal.

This superb away win was achieved without England captain David Beckham, who suffered a hamstring injury in the Bernabeu, but there was little sign of the goal-scoring carnage to come when Jenas fired Newcastle in front with a spectacular strike after 20 minutes. Barthez saved Craig Bellamy's initial effort but Jenas pounced on the loose ball to lash it high into the top corner of the net.

As the BBC reported, 'It was the signal for a spell of champagne football from United – illustrated by a devastating spell of three goals in 5 minutes.'

An exquisite pass by Giggs sent Solskjaer clear to equalise, but it was a double strike by Scholes that wrecked Newcastle's hopes of gaining anything from the game, while at the same time virtually extinguishing their title hopes with just five games remaining.

The midfielder exchanged passes with Solskjaer before volleying the ball past Given for his first goal and then smashed in a superb long-range drive into the top corner for his second after another mesmerising run from Giggs, aided by Wes Brown.

Giggs himself then turned from provider to scorer 2 minutes before the interval, tucking the ball past Given from close range after John O'Shea had struck the bar having neatly tricked both Nolberto Solano and Aaron Hughes.

The second half started with Diego Forlan on for hamstring victim Giggs – but there was no respite for Newcastle from the merciless visitors.

Scholes completed a deserved hat-trick from close range after substitute Gary Neville (on for O'Shea) had carved out an opening, and with leading scorer van Nistelrooy seemingly having a quiet game, the Dutchman stepped up to fire home a penalty on 59 minutes after the hapless Titus Bramble senselessly felled Forlan inside the area.

As St James' Park emptied rapidly, and Roy Keane hobbled off with a leg injury, a surprised Shola Ameobi took advantage of an error by United goalkeeper Barthez to score a second for the outclassed home side, who even had Alan Shearer booked by efficient referee Steve Dunn.

'This was one heck of a win,' said Alex Ferguson after the game, while Giggs added; 'We played some terrific football ... let's hope we can reproduce a similar display against Arsenal and then Real Madrid.'

United drew 2-2 with the Gunners in the vital Premier League game and then beat Blackburn Rovers 3-1 before taking on Real Madrid in the second leg of their Champions League quarter-final.

Results continued to go United's way in the League and, following Arsenal's surprise 3-2 home defeat by Leeds on 4 May, they were declared champions for the eighth time.

34

Manchester United 4 Real Madrid 3
Champions League, Quarter-Final, 2nd Leg
23 April 2003

United's trio of Ryan Giggs, Roy Keane and John O'Shea were all passed fit to start against the Spanish Galacticos but Paul Scholes was absent. Sebastian Veron came into midfield and Wes Brown was preferred at right-back but David Beckham was left on the bench!

Striker Raúl and Conceicao were missing from the Real line-up who, after gaining a 3-1 lead in the first leg, were clear favourites to go through to the semi-finals.

United, of course, had produced some excellent performances in the Champions League, including that superb 3-0 win over Juventus in Italy and 2-0 and 2-1 victories over the 2002 beaten finalists Bayer Leverkusen from Germany.

Of the previous seven competitive meetings with Real Madrid, United had managed just one win (1-0 in the European Cup of 1968); they had drawn three and lost three, conceding three goals in each of their defeats.

So the scene was set, and with a galaxy of stars out on the pitch and a certain Roman Abramovich watching from the stands, presumably falling in love with football, this would turn out to be a night to remember for a lot of reasons!

Manchester United (4-4-2): Barthez; Brown, Ferdinand, Silvestre (P. Neville), O'Shea, Keane (Fortune), Butt, Veron (Beckham), Giggs, Solskjaer, van Nistelrooy.
Real Madrid (4-2-1-1): Casillas; Michel Salgado, Heirro, Roberto Carlos, Helguera, Guti, Makelele, Figo (Pavon), Zidane, McManaman (Portillo), Ronaldo (Solari).
Attendance: 66,708

Surprisingly, the crowd inside Old Trafford was 1,500 below capacity, but those present saw a cracking game of football. And in the end Ferguson's drastically revised strategy was justified, as United claimed victory over the reigning European champions on the night – which was outstanding, but sadly not enough to secure overall glory.

Needing to win 3-0 at least (even 3-1, 4-2 or 5-3, to take the tie into extra time and then penalties), United gave it all and almost claimed a famous overall victory.

Beckham's cameo appearance as a 63rd minute substitute brought him two goals and his presence on the field certainly had an impact during the last third of the game when United almost turned what was to be a memorable 4-3 win in the end into an Easter miracle. It didn't quite happen, but they came mighty close!

Only the hat-trick scored by Brazilian striker Ronaldo stopped United from pulling off a terrific two-legged win.

One might say that had Beckham started the game, things might well have been different. We will never know but suffice to say, as soon as 'Golden Balls' entered the fray, the Spaniards looked worried, and more so after he had netted twice!

Beckham had played in the first leg in Madrid where Roberto Carlos had the better of their mano-a-mano duel down the flank. But when Beckham came on this time, it was a different ball game.

Early in this second-leg contest, the United fans roared when John O'Shea slipped the ball through Luis Figo's legs but that excitement quickly subsided when, in the 12th minute, Ronaldo struck his first blow.

It looked as if the World Cup-winning striker had far too much to do as he chased after Guti's long pass, leaving Rio Ferdinand in his wake. Not at all. The Brazilian let fly with a powerful right-foot shot past United's goalkeeper, Fabien Barthez.

For a while United found it hard to get hold of the ball, just as it was in the first leg, but once Ruud van Nistelrooy, Ryan Giggs and Ole Gunnar Solskjaer got into their stride, the visitors' defence looked vulnerable.

At last United, with the crowd behind them, started to play and slowly but surely they began to put pressure on Real's goal.

After a series of worthy attacks, they deservedly equalised just 2 minutes before the half-time whistle. A wonderful pass by Giggs found Solskjaer who, looking up, drove the ball across the Real goal towards van Nistelrooy who delivered the killer blow.

After the interval, United continued to pour forward in numbers, but were caught on the break as the elegant Zidane set up Figo whose clever chip bounced off United's crossbar with Barthez a mere spectator.

Zidane split United's defence for a second time in the 50th minute and on this occasion it resulted in another goal for Ronaldo, who was in the right position at the right time to steer Roberto Carlos's cross into the net from close range.

Stunned United hit back immediately and, to their credit, within 2 minutes they were once again on level terms, but at 5-3 behind on aggregate they still had an enormous mountain to climb.

The equalising goal came after Sebastian Veron, who was finding it tough going in midfield, tried a speculative, yet harmless looking, long-range shot which Ivan Helguera somehow diverted past his own keeper, Casillas who certainly tore a strip of his team-mate!

Veron then forced a fine save from Casillas, but in the 59th minute the brilliant Ronaldo struck again, this time beating Barthez with a stunning drive from 28 yards after being given far too much room by the United defence. But what goal it was ... one of the best seen at Old Trafford for year. Even Ryan Giggs applauded it.

Behind again on the night and needing a miracle to go through to the semi-finals, Ferguson had no choice but to take off Veron and send on Beckham.

And within 8 minutes it was 3-3 as Beckham found the back of Casillas' net with a trademark free-kick.

It was all United at this point in the game and after Giggs had shot wide and van Nistelrooy came close with a header, Beckham notched his second goal in the 84th minute to edge the Reds in front.

Some clever and astute play by van Nistelrooy enabled the Dutchman to fire in a low shot which Casillas failed to hold. Beckham, following up, was able to nudge the ball over the line from a couple of feet. 4-3 … it was now game on. But United needed to score again to take tie into extra time. Everyone poured forward and if there was a kitchen sink around, that would have been tossed into the mix as well.

In a dramatic climax to a thoroughly entertaining game, United just couldn't manage another goal and at the final whistle there was bitter disappointment on the face of manager Ferguson and his team.

Real had given United an education lesson on how to play football in Madrid … and at times they did exactly the same at Old Trafford. Giggs said after the game, 'Phew, that was some match. We did our best but on the night it just wasn't enough. There'll be another day, I'm sure.'

N.B. Some pundits rate this as one of the 'best' European Cup games ever staged at Old Trafford. And Giggsy is one who totally agrees.

35

Manchester United 3 Millwall 0
FA Cup Final
22 May 2004

On their way to the Millennium Stadium in Cardiff, United defeated Aston Villa, Northampton Town, arch-rivals Manchester City (4-2 at Old Trafford), Fulham and Arsenal, while underdogs Millwall, who had finished a moderate tenth in League Division Two, had eliminated Walsall, Telford United, Burnley, Tranmere Rovers and Sunderland.

With three defeats in their last six Premier League games, United's form hadn't been great, but manager Alex Ferguson was confident his players 'would perform on the day' while his counterpart Dennis Wise had seen his team win only twice in ten starts since late March.

This was Millwall's first ever appearance in an FA Cup final – their best effort prior to this encounter was to reach the semi-final stage in 1900, 1903 and 1937, the latter as a Third Division (S) club.

Manchester United (4-4-1-1): Howard (Carroll); G. Neville, Brown, Silvestre, O'Shea, Ronaldo (Solskjaer), Fletcher (Butt), Keane, Giggs, Scholes, van Nistelrooy.
Millwall (4-4-2): Marshall; Ryan (Cogan), Ward, Lawrence, Elliott, Sweeney, Livermore, Wise (Weston), Ifill, Cahill, Harris (McCammon).
Attendance: 72,350

Two key midfield players – United's Roy Keane and Millwall's Wise – overcame their injury problems to make the final. And it was Keane who was first into the action with a hefty challenge on David Livermore.

Cristiano Ronaldo, wearing gold-coloured boots, showed his trickery against nineteen-year-old Robbie Ryan and an early thrust by the Portuguese international almost caught the Lions out. His incisive runs would hurt Millwall time and again with the aforementioned full-back Ryan bearing the brunt of the winger's repertoire of skills.

Millwall, in fact, settled down quickest, enjoying plenty of early touches as United struggled to get the ball.

But it didn't take Alex Ferguson's team long to unveil their attacking threat.

On 4 minutes, Ronaldo crossed from the right, only for Ruud van Nistelrooy to send his diving header narrowly wide of Andy Marshall's goal.

More creative work from the impressive Ronaldo exposed Millwall again shortly afterwards, and from his tempting cross the ball broke to Paul Scholes, who failed to connect from 6 yards.

Marshall then produced a brilliant one-handed from Keane's swerving long-range strike. It was all United as Millwall's defence came under ever more pressure, but they held firm, just, as Ryan Giggs, Ruud van Nistelrooy and Darren Fletcher all had efforts charged down.

With United on the front foot, and half-time looming, Marshall half-saved a shot from Ronaldo but Darren Ward was in the right position to hack the ball off the line.

But Ronaldo's superb first-half display was eventually rewarded with a goal 3 minutes before the interval.

United's midfielders switched the ball from left to right, before Gary Neville's looping cross was headed home by Ronaldo at the far post.

The goal was hard on Millwall, who had blunted United's attacking threat pretty well, while also enjoying some good spells of their own.

Almost immediately after the goal, a cleverly taken short corner almost caught United out and it took a timely punch by keeper Tim Howard, off Tim Cahill's head, to clear the danger before Paul Ifill had a shot blocked.

As the players left the pitch at half-time, player/manager Wise tangled with Scholes, but Cleveland referee Jeff Winter opted for a cautionary word with both players and ensured Wise left the field without further harming his team's cause.

Early in the second half, a driving run from Fletcher signalled United's determination to take the game beyond Millwall and within minutes Marshall had to save from Scholes who looked certain to score a killer second goal.

Mikael Silvestre almost scored from United's tenth corner of the match, but Wise brilliantly headed the ball off the line before Ryan booted it to safety.

The decisive second goal finally arrived in the 64th minute and in emphatic style too.

Giggs went on a jinking run into the Lions' penalty area where Livermore brought him down. Up stepped van Nistelrooy to smash the spot kick home for his twenty-ninth goal of the season.

After more United pressure when Giggs (twice), substitute Ole Gunnar Solskjaer and Scholes all tested Marshall, the prolific Dutchman was in place to score a third goal on 80 minutes, sliding the ball home after some more excellent work by the impressive Giggs.

With time running out and the game sewed up, Ferguson brought on goalkeeper Roy Carroll to give him a slice of the glory.

Millwall also had time to make a significant substitution – bringing on Curtis Weston, who became the youngest ever FA Cup finalist at the age of seventeen years and 119 days.

Ronaldo, often pilloried by critics for over-playing, was by far the game's outstanding footballer, but Giggs wasn't too far behind him. 'He was a joy to watch at times,' said his manager.

For United, this was their eleventh FA Cup final triumph, two more than Arsenal, and it certainly made up for a disappointing season which saw them finish third in the Premier League while lifting the FA Community Shield (on penalties).

36

Manchester United 4 Wigan Athletic 0
League Cup Final
26 February 2006

Having been knocked out of the FA Cup by Liverpool just eight days earlier, United were in no mood to lose this final against a Wigan side who had already ousted Bournemouth, Watford, Newcastle United, Bolton Wanderers and Arsenal.

United, who had eliminated Barnet, West Bromwich Albion, Birmingham City and Blackburn Rovers, had lost only two of their previous sixteen Premier League games, and they had already whipped Wigan 4-0 in a League game at Old Trafford. They were in good form, whereas the Latics had recorded only one league win in eight yet were lying seventh in the table, whereas United were second.

For United this was their sixth League Cup final, for Wigan it was their first ever final in a major competition, although they had lifted both the Freight Rover Trophy and Auto Windscreen Shield in 1985 and 1999 respectively.

Manchester United (4-4-2): Van der Sar; G. Neville, Ferdinand, Brown (Vidic), Silvestre (Evra), Park, O'Shea, Giggs, Ronaldo, Rooney, Saha.
Wigan Athletic (4-1-3-2): Pollitt (Filan); Chimbomda, Henchoz (McCulloch), Teale, De Zueew, Baines, Bullard, Kavanagh (Ziegler), Scharner, Camara, Roberts.
Attendance: 66,866

The Guardian reporter Kevin McCarra wrote,

There will be discussion over the memorability of this Carling Cup success, but Manchester United unquestionably made this a match to forget for Wigan Athletic. Getting to Cardiff was immeasurably more pleasurable than being there on the end of a record margin of defeat for the final of this competition since the two-legged format was abandoned.

While this contest provided little true corroboration of Sir Alex Ferguson's claim that he has a young team that will flourish in a couple of years, the players certainly imitated the stance of celebrated predecessors at United. They established their superiority with a flourish.

With Louis Saha up front in place of Ruud van Nistelrooy, United attacked from the off, going at the Latics with a specific purpose. Wigan, who had gone ten games without a clean sheet, looked ponderous at the back with United looking dangerous every time they went forward.

After gaining a 1-0 half-time lead, United easily coped with a short-lived revival from Wigan before scoring three more goals in the space of 5 minutes leading up to the hour mark.

Cristiano Ronaldo, who of course had scored on this same ground in United's FA Cup final win over Millwall the previous year, was once again in outstanding form.

Unfortunately Wigan's goalkeeper, Mike Pollitt, damaged his hamstring while fielding the ball in the opening exchanges and had to go off in the 14th minute.

His replacement, John Filan, was in the firing line immediately and after intense United pressure, during which time Ronaldo fluffed Rooney's cut-back, Wigan fell behind in the 33rd minute.

Edwin van der Sar's kick downfield was nodded on by the lively Saha and, as Arjan de Zeeuw collided with his teammate Pascal Chimbonda, Rooney darted into the gap to place his low shot beyond Filan for his first goal since 28 December.

Wigan started the second half much better and in the 51st minute Henri Camara got past Rio Ferdinand but his shot was blocked by Van der Sar. However, 4 minutes later, Giggs switched play to the right, Ronaldo fed the overlapping Gary Neville and, although Saha failed to convert the full-back's cross, the ball bounced off Filan, back onto the French striker and into the net.

Stéphane Henchoz then hit an attempted clearance straight to Saha, who put Ronaldo through for United's third. Almost immediately, Wigan conceded again. The defence failed to clear a menacing Giggs free kick and the unmarked Ferdinand headed down for Rooney to turn and steer the ball past Filan.

Manager Ferguson had once again watched his men conduct themselves purposefully on the field of play as he collected his first trophy since 2004 and fueled the argument that he should remain in charge at Old Trafford to direct the quest for more honours. And why not, especially with Ryan Giggs in the team!

37

Manchester United 4 Blackburn Rovers 1
Premier League
31 March 2007

Going into this game, United had a six-point advantage over Chelsea at the top of the Premier League, having suffered only one defeat in their previous thirteen League games. They were also fresh from a 4-1 home victory over Lancashire rivals Bolton Wanderers, and with games fast running out they knew they had to keep on winning, simply because their closest challengers from London were also in good form.

Edwin Van der Sar, who had missed the Bolton game, was back between the posts in place of Tomasz Kuszczak (on loan from West Bromwich Albion) while Wes Brown took over from Gary Neville at right-back and Paul Scholes returned to midfield after suspension.

Mid-table Blackburn, managed by former United star Mark Hughes, had lost five of their previous eight League games and were without the suspended David Bentley.

Manchester United (4-3-2-1): Van der Sar; Brown, Ferdinand, Vidic (O'Shea 28), Heinze, Ronaldo (Solskjaer), Carrick, Scholes, Park, Giggs (Smith), Rooney.
Blackburn Rovers (4-4-1-1): Friedel; Emerton, Samba, Nelsen, Warnock, Dunn, Kerimoglu (Peter), Mokoena, Pedersen, Derbyshire, McCarthy (Roberts).
Attendance: 76,098

A record crowd inside the redesigned and reconstructed Old Trafford Stadium saw United come back from a goal down to beat plucky Blackburn Rovers and take a giant step nearer to their ninth Premier League title.

United weren't at their best in the first half, but after the break they were magnificent!

From the moment Rovers' former England U21 international Matt Derbyshire gave the visitors a shock lead in the 29th minute, the Theatre of Dreams became a cauldron of noise which Sir Alex Ferguson later described as 'the best atmosphere in years'.

United dug deep and Paul Scholes equalised with a cracking effort just after the hour mark before fellow midfielder Michael Carrick deliberately side-footed the ball through a gap in a crowded penalty area to edge United 2-1 in front on 73 minutes. And it was effectively game over when Park Ji-Sung pounced to slide in United's third goal. With 7 minutes remaining, and with Merseyside referee Chris Foy looking at his watch, Ole Gunnar Solskjaer put the icing on the cake by driving in United's fourth goal.

David Dunn and Derbyshire had early half-chances for Rovers, but it was United who had the first clear opportunity, though Cristiano Ronaldo's strike was blocked by goalkeeper Brad Friedel. The ball fell loose for Wayne Rooney and he thought he had found the net only for the American to scramble across his line and palm his effort wide.

Rovers had a penalty appeal turned down when the ball struck Wes Brown's arm before the lack of form and confidence Rooney had been showing for England transferred itself to club level. Finding himself unmarked at the far post, and with only Friedel to beat, he failed to connect properly with Ryan Giggs' cross and then saw his second attempt smothered by the Blackburn keeper. The agony etched the striker's face was plain for all to see, although he did get a pat on the back from Giggs.

Unfortunately, United's central defender Nemanja Vidic was then forced off with a broken collarbone. A stalwart in United's defence, he fell awkwardly when challenging for a header at a corner.

United barely had time to settle before Derbyshire gave Blackburn the lead with a poacher's goal. Carrick diverted a Morten Gamst Pedersen cross towards his own net and, despite keeper Edwin van der Sar saving, Derbyshire was on the spot to side-foot the ball high into the roof of the net.

United piled on the pressure and, in fact, they bombarded the Rovers' goal for a good 15 minutes up to half-time, Giggs, Rooney and Park all going close to equalising.

They continued in the same vein at the start of the second period but Rovers' back division held firm, just!

One can sense that the home fans were getting frustrated and so too was Rio Ferdinand, who kicked the ball into the crowd and hit a spectator when referee Foy refused to play advantage when United were charging towards the Rovers' goal.

After a series of quick-fire attacks, eventually Blackburn caved in! Scholes wriggled into space in the area and drove home a low shot past the gallant Friedel on 61 minutes.

Then, with Rovers on the back foot and shortly after Giggs had seen his effort come back off the crossbar from just 8 yards out, Carrick spared the Welshman's blushes with an angled shot which gave Friedel no chance. United were in front and in control.

Park scored a third goal from point-blank range after being the quickest to react after Friedel had parried a Ronaldo free kick, and to round things off Solskjaer added the finishing touch to the win with his late strike.

Once again, Giggs had a fine game for the Reds. The Welsh ace nearing a personal milestone of 500 League appearances (this would come on the 17 April *v.* Sheffield United), having already played in his 700th senior game for the club on 21 January at Arsenal, had a fine game; so too did Carrick. And this solid victory left United, who also had a vastly superior goal-difference, six points clear of Chelsea at the top of the table with seven games remaining. And they still had to play each other at Stamford Bridge.

After this victory over Blackburn, Joe Bernstein wrote in the *Daily Mail*: 'If United go on to claim their ninth Premier League title in fifteen years, outstanding goals from Scholes and Carrick will become part of club folklore.'

United, as predicted by many, went on to claim the championship. They drew their crucial game at Chelsea 0-0 and then celebrated after Jose Mourinho's side could only draw with Arsenal in their penultimate match of the season, allowing United to finish six points clear (89-83). And at this point the Reds were still in the Champions League and there was the small matter of an FA Cup final with no other than Chelsea.

N.B. This game is included because of the record Old Trafford attendance.

38

Manchester United 7 AS Roma 1
(United won 8-3 on aggregate)
Champions League Quarter-Final, 2nd Leg
10 April 2007

After beating Blackburn Rovers at the end of March, United suffered a 2-1 defeat in the first leg of their Champions League quarter-final tie away to AS Roma in front of almost 75,000 fans inside the Stadio Olimpico, before surprisingly going down 2-1 at Portsmouth and then beating Sheffield United 2-0 at Old Trafford in Premier League matches.

Their form hadn't been great in these three matches and manager Alex Ferguson admitted 'I am not happy', but insisted that his players would certainly pull out the stops against the Italians.

On their way to the last eight, United had won and lost against Celtic (3-2 and 0-1), beat Benfica twice (3-1 and 1-0) and had been victorious and suffered defeat against FC Copenhagen (3-0 and 0-1) in Group F before defeating Lille 2-0 on aggregate in the first knockout round.

AS Roma (with three wins, two defeats and a draw) had finished second behind Valencia in Group D before eliminating Lyon 2-0 on aggregate in their knockout round tie. Brazilian goalkeeper Doni, Francesco Totti, Daniele De Rossi and David 'Pek' Pizarro were the stars of their team under manager Luciano Spalletti.

Manchester United (4-4-2): Van der Sar; Brown, Ferdinand, O'Shea (Evra), Heinze, Carrick (Richardson), Ronaldo, Fletcher, Giggs (Solskjaer), Smith, Rooney.

AS Roma (4-4-1-1): Doni; Panucci, Cassetti, Mexes, Chivo, De Rossi (Faty), Wilhelmsson (Rosi), Vucinic, Mancini (Okaka Chuka), Totti, Pizarro.

Attendance: 74,476

Well, no one expected this ... not even Ryan Giggs!

Having lost the first leg in Italy, albeit narrowly, United knew they had to be at their best to overcome the Serie A side who at the time were lying second in their domestic League behind Inter Milan.

After referee Lubos Michel from Slovakia had got the game underway, both sides immediately showed attacking intentions and, in the opening few minutes, Roma's Francesco Totti came close to putting his side in front with a fierce shot that fizzed past Edwin van der Sar's right-hand post.

But it was United – roared on by the fans – who grabbed control of the tie with three goals in the space of just eight first-half minutes to stun the Italians.

Michael Carrick opened the scoring on 11 minutes. He collected a shrewd pass from Cristiano Ronaldo and, taking his time, he bent ball past the stationary figure of Doni.

6 minutes later, with Roma's defence at sixes and sevens, United went 2-0 in front, and 3-2 ahead on aggregate.

Gabriel Heinze and the lively Ryan Giggs combined down the left before the Welshman flighted a perfect pass into the path of Alan Smith, who finished with great precision – his first goal for United since November 2005!

Next up, it was Wayne Rooney who got in on the act in the 19th minute. Looking for space, he timed his run superbly to slot home Giggs' low cross after the Italian side had been completely torn apart down the right flank.

A shell-shocked Roma tried to respond and almost pulled a goal back when Philippe Mexes headed a David Pizarro free kick a yard or so wide. But the visitors' attempts to claw themselves back into the game only succeeded in leaving themselves vulnerable at the back and United, with their quick-fire attack, capitalised to the full.

Carrick went close when he headed a swinging corner by Giggs directly at Doni but the midfielder couldn't react quick enough when the ball bounced straight back to him.

The sprightly Ronaldo, who at times was causing Roma plenty of problems, made it 4-0 before half-time with a precise finish into the bottom corner of Doni's net after two visiting defenders had made the big mistake of inviting him to shoot. Never do that!

United were now playing exquisite football; they were simply superb, and they continued to batter hapless Roma after the break with Giggs at his brilliant best.

Ronaldo, who was also in sublime form, slid home a low Giggs cross for number five before Carrick belted home a real pile-driver to make 6-0 on the hour mark.

Perhaps surprisingly, Roma pulled a goal back through De Rossi, who beat Van der Sar with a neat finish on the turn, but the game was long since up for the Italian side.

United were now playing to the gallery … it was exhibition stuff without a shadow of doubt for Ferguson's side, who were making Roma look horribly bad, and as the game was drawing to a close, United grabbed a seventh goal, richly deserved, when substitute Patrice Evra's low shot beat Doni.

Like United's first six goals it was a fine finish and completed a magnificent victory, their biggest in Europe since they beat Irish side Waterford en route to winning the European Cup in 1968.

After this emphatic victory, United faced another Serie A side, AC Milan, in the semi-final, but after registering a 3-2 first leg victory at Old Trafford they were well beaten 3-0 in Italy to go out 5-3 on aggregate. AC Milan went on to beat Liverpool 2-1 in the final in Athens.

N.B. There have been many memorable performances at Old Trafford down the years but few can compare to the display Sir Alex Ferguson's men put on against AS Roma in 2007. It was brilliant, absolutely brilliant.

39

Manchester United 0 Chelsea 1
(after extra time)
FA Cup Final
19 May 2007

Ahead of José Mourinho's first FA Cup final as the manager of Chelsea, it was reported that up to five players could miss what, to some, would be perhaps one of the greatest occasions of their footballing careers.

As for Ryan Giggs, it was to be his seventh FA Cup final, equalling Roy Keane's post-war record, having played in the 1994, 1995, 1996, 1999, 2004 and 2005 finals.

The 2007 clash between the Blues and the Reds was the eighth FA Cup final in a row involving a London club: Arsenal (four appearances), Chelsea (two), and Millwall and West Ham United (one each) had all been involved since the Manchester United-Newcastle contest in 1999.

The bookies were undecided as to who would be the eventual winners, but United were full of confidence, having knocked out Aston Villa 2-1, Portsmouth 2-1, Reading 3-2, Middlesbrough 1-0 (in a replay) and Watford 4-1.

Chelsea, meanwhile, had reached the final by scoring a total of twenty goals. They started by hammering hapless Macclesfield Town 6-1 before ousting Nottingham Forest 3-1, Norwich City 4-0, Tottenham Hotspur 2-1(in a replay after a 3-3 draw) and Blackburn Rovers, also by 2-1.

Before the kick-off, there was an official opening ceremony of the new Wembley Stadium with Prince William doing the honours, as well as a fly-past by the famous Red Arrows, plus a parade on the pitch of former FA Cup winners (players), including the Chelsea duo of Ron Harris (1970 captain) and Marcel Desailly (2000) and the Manchester United octet of Denis Law (1963), Lou Macari (1977), Arthur Albiston (1983), Norman Whiteside (1985), Lee Martin (1990), Mark Hughes (1994), Gary Pallister (1996) and Peter Schmeichel (1999).

Chelsea (4-4-1-1): Čech; Ferriera, Essien, Terry, Bridge, Makelele, Lampard, Mikel, J. Cole (Robben/A. Cole), Wright-Phillips (Kalou), Drogba.
Manchester United (4-4-2): Van der Sar; Brown, Ferdinand, Vidic, Heinz, Carrick (O'Shea), Scholes, Fletcher (Smith), Giggs (Solskjaer), Ronaldo, Rooney.
Attendance: 89,826

Referee Steve Bennett (Kent) got the game underway in front of almost 90,000 fans – the biggest attendance for an FA Cup final since Wimbledon's unexpected 1-0 victory over Liverpool in 1988, when the turnout was 98,203.

Chelsea, aiming to become only the third team to achieve the domestic cup double (after Arsenal in 1993 and Liverpool in 2001) started well, but it has to be said that the opening 20 minutes were marked by cautious play and a lack of creativity from both teams.

On 21 minutes Didier Drogba produced the game's first noticeable attempt on goal – hammering a low shot wide from some 30 yards. 10 minutes later, Chelsea's Frank Lampard forced a save from United's Dutch goalkeeper Edwin van der Sar.

Wayne Rooney, playing well up field, was twice caught offside as United pushed forward, but the closest they came in the first half was a long-distance effort by the aforementioned striker.

At half time, Chelsea boss José Mourinho made a like-for-like substitution, bringing on winger Arjen Robben for Joe Cole, but before the spectators had taken their seats in the 'posh area' Rooney produced the most exciting action of the game, dribbling round two defenders, only to see his powerful shot saved by Petr Čech.

10 minutes later, Rooney was in action again, carrying the ball some 60 yards towards the Chelsea penalty area, only to be tackled by the last Chelsea defender, Wayne Bridge. It was all United at this point; Chelsea were on the back foot and after Ryan Giggs flashed a volley barely two feet over the bar from close range, United's Paul Scholes picked up the game's first booking for a foul on Lampard.

From the resulting free kick, Drogba curled the ball round United's wall and off the outside of Van der Sar's post. Soon afterwards, the lively Rooney, after a mazy dribble, was denied by the alert Čech, who snatched the ball off the England striker's foot.

With neither side doing enough to score during the scheduled 90-plus minutes, an FA Cup final went into extra time for the third consecutive year.

And it was United who had the next chance, but Giggs, only 3 yards out, failed to get proper contact on the ball and Čech was down to make the save – or did he?

Giggs appealed for a goal, claiming that the ball had crossed the line while in Čech's arms, but the linesman's flag stayed down and play was waved on. However, television replays appeared to show that the ball did cross the line, but only after Giggs's momentum had pushed the Chelsea keeper backwards into his own goal!

Also, after the game, United manager Sir Alex Ferguson claimed that Giggs had been fouled by Essien just before he took his shot.

The deadlock was finally broken in the 116th minute when Drogba played a one-two with Lampard on the edge of the United penalty-area after receiving the ball from John Obi Mikel. Although losing his balance, the big striker was still able to prod it past the onrushing Van der Sar and into the net.

Chelsea picked up three more bookings in the last few minutes as they fought off a late United challenge, but in the end it was Drogba's goal which decided a tight contest and, as the blue half of Wembley celebrated, the Red section, along with Giggs and his teammates, looked on somewhat dejected.

40

Manchester United 2 Wigan Athletic 0
Premier League
11 May 2008

Everyone associated with Manchester United – and millions of football enthusiasts worldwide – knew that victory in this, their final League game of the season, against Wigan Athletic, managed by former Old Trafford favourite Steve Bruce, would clinch a tenth Premier League title for Sir Alex Ferguson's men.

At the time of kick-off at the JJB Stadium, United had accumulated eighty-four points, the same number as a second-placed Chelsea, but United's goal-difference was vastly superior. If both teams drew, then of course United would take the crown but that was not an option!

'We will go out a win,' said Fergie, and Ryan Giggs backed him up, saying: 'This is a big, big match. It will be tough, we all know that, but we're confident and we will certainly not be complacent.'

On this same afternoon, Chelsea were at home to sixteenth placed Bolton Wanderers, and were expected to win!

Nemanja Vidic and Wayne Rooney, both of whom had missed United's previous game (a 4-1 home win over West Ham) were back in the starting line-up. Giggs was on the bench for the second game running, but ready and eager to equal the club's appearance record. Wigan, 2-0 winners at Aston Villa in their previous game when future United star Antonio Valencia netted twice, were missing left-wing back Kevin Kilbane, but Emile Heskey and Marcus Bent were fit to start up front.

Wigan Athletic (4-4-2): Kirkland, Boyce, Bramble, Scharner, Figueroa, Valencia, Palacios, Brown (King), Koumas, Bent (Sibierski), Heskey.
Manchester United (4-4-2): Van der Sar, Brown, Ferdinand, Vidic, Evra, Ronaldo, Carrick, Scholes (Hargreaves), Park (Giggs), Tevez, Rooney.
Attendance: 25,133

Right from the start United were on the front foot, but Wigan, up for the fight, defended stubbornly, denying the visitors space in all areas of the field. But gradually United gained control in midfield and it came as no surprise when Cristiano Ronaldo opened the scoring from the penalty spot on 33 minutes, awarded by Kent referee Steve Bennett after Emmerson had fouled Rooney.

After Heskey had wasted Wigan's best chance with a second-half header, substitute Giggs clinched victory with a cool finish from Rooney's pass 10 minutes from time.

This all-important and match-clinching goal sent Alex Ferguson dancing down the touchline in the pouring rain, knowing at the time that Chelsea were leading Bolton by a goal to nil.

It was also a very special occasion for Giggs who, when entering the play in the 68th minute, equalled United's appearance record of 758 games, held at the time by Sir Bobby Charlton, who was watching the game from the directors' box.

Charlton was equally elated and made his way to the tunnel to embrace Giggs after the final whistle, thousands of ecstatic United supporters inside the JJB celebrated a second successive title as a jubilant and delighted Giggs lifted the Premier League trophy.

The next milestone for Giggs was to overtake Charlton's club record of 606 League appearances, and he achieved that against Liverpool at Anfield on 6 March 2011, having equalled the record against Chelsea five days earlier.

Back to the match itself ... and Wigan certainly put up fierce resistance before United made their superiority tell when it mattered.

It was a good contest overall with Wigan proving more than a match in a closely fought first half.

Paul Scholes was booked for a wild challenge on Wilson Palacios as United fought to establish a foothold, and it was the midfielder who had the first shot, sending a 20-yarder wide.

After Boyce had wasted a half-chance, Wigan were denied what looked to be a clear penalty after 22 minutes when Rio Ferdinand seemed to block Jason Koumas's shot with his upper arm. And Wigan's frustration increased 11 minutes later when United were awarded a spot-kick after Rooney had fallen to the ground under Boyce's challenge. Ronaldo sent Chris Kirkland the wrong way with the minimum of fuss.

Scholes was then let off by referee Bennett after blatantly blocking a run by Wilson Palacios. The crowd waited for the red card but the United midfielder received only a stern lecture. Wrong decision.

The second half began in a deluge, with the pitch becoming treacherous, and Ronaldo tested Kirkland with a rising 30-yard free kick which the keeper turned over the top.

On 52 minutes Wigan got a stroke of luck when Scholes was hacked down by Titus Bramble, but this time referee Bennett and his assistant ignored United's claims for a spot-kick.

United were more impressive after the interval and as they went in search of the second goal, Kirkland saved superbly from Rooney, following up soon afterwards with a crucial stop from Carlos Tevez's deflected shot.

With around a quarter of the game remaining, Owen Hargreaves and Giggs came on in quick succession, but before either player got into the game Heskey saw his header miss the target by inches.

With 10 minutes left for play United, who were now in full control, scored a second goal and appropriately it was Giggs who delivered the killer blow, clinching the Premier League title. Taking Rooney's clever pass in his stride, the Welshman slid the ball home in a composed fashion from 12 yards.

This second goal, plus a late equaliser for Bolton at Chelsea, sparked scenes of wild celebrations among the United fans. It was a joyous occasion for all.

Next up, in ten days' time, was the Champions League final against Chelsea in Moscow. The double was on and United were in the right frame at the right time. Russia here we come.

41

Manchester United 1 Chelsea 1
(after extra time, United won 6-5 on penalties)
Champions League Final
21 May 2008

Both United and Chelsea had to battle through twelve games on their way to the final.

United were unbeaten, defeating two teams twice in Group F – Dynamo Kiev (4-2 and 4-0) and Sporting Lisbon (1-0 and 2-1). They also beat and drew with AS Roma (1-0 and 1-1) in their group before eliminating Lyon 2-1 on aggregate in the first knockout stage. Facing AS Roma again in the quarter-finals, United were far too good for the Serie A side and recorded a 3-0 overall victory to secure a semi-final match with FC Barcelona. After a tough battle in front of almost 96,000 fans inside the Camp Nou, which ended 0-0, United won 1-0 at Old Trafford to reach the final. Ryan Giggs came on as a late substitute in both games against the Spanish giants.

Chelsea had lost one of their dozen matches, succumbing 2-1 away to Fenerbahce in their quarter-final tie before winning the return leg 2-0 at Stamford Bridge. Then the Blues knocked out Liverpool in the semi-final 4-3 on aggregate.

So, the scene was set for the big showdown in Russia. United, who had clinched the Premier League title ten days earlier, were in a very confident mood, while Chelsea, runner's-up in the League, had already lost one final, beaten 2-1 by London rivals Tottenham Hotspur in the League Cup. And there had already been three meetings between United and Chelsea earlier in the season. The Community Shield encounter finished level at 1-1 and both clubs won the respective home Premier League game.

This was the first ever all-English European Cup/Champions League final and it was only the third time that two clubs from the same country had contested the final; the others being the Real Madrid v. Valencia battle in 2000 and the AC Milan v. Juventus contest in 2003. It was also the first European Cup final played in Russia, and hence the easternmost final in the tournament's history. It also marked the 100th anniversary of Manchester United's first ever League triumph, the fiftieth anniversary of the Munich air disaster, and the fiftieth anniversary of United's first European Cup triumph in 1968. And it was United's third European Cup final, the other coming in 1999, while for Chelsea it was their first.

Chelsea (4-3-1-2): Čech, Essien, Carvalho, Terry, Ashley Cole, Ballack, Makelele (Belletti), Lampard, Joe Cole (Anelka), Drogba, Malouda (Kalou).
Manchester United (4-4-2): Van der Sar, Brown (Anderson), Ferdinand, Vidic, Evra, Hargreaves, Scholes (Giggs), Carrick, Ronaldo, Tevez, Rooney (Nani).
Attendance: 69,552

The opening exchanges of this eagerly anticipated Champions League final amounted to little more than sparring, but the game suddenly burst into life after 20 minutes following an aerial collision between Paul Scholes and Claude Makelele. Both players were yellow-carded by referee Lubos Michel of Slovakia and the United midfielder walked away with a bloody nose.

Cristiano Ronaldo, who had started to give Michael Essien a torrid time, burst onto the scene in style in the 26th minute, soaring highest above the Chelsea defence to head home his forty-second goal of the season from Wes Brown's cross.

7 minutes later, Chelsea came close to an equaliser but alert goalkeeper Van der Sar clawed away a header from his own defender, Rio Ferdinand, after Didier Drogba had forced Frank Lampard's dangerous cross into the 6-yard box.

Then, in the 34th minute, after a swift-flowing 80-yard move from one penalty area to the other, Van der Sar's opposite number Petr Čech denied United a second goal with a brilliant double save. Wayne Rooney found Ronaldo with a sweeping pass, and from his delivery Carlos Tevez saw his header blocked by Čech, who then recovered to make a magnificent one-handed stop from Michael Carrick's follow-up effort.

Tevez was denied again 4 minutes before the interval when, after escaping the attentions of Makelele, he was just short as he slid in towards Rooney's low centre.

However, with the half-time whistle imminent, United were pegged back.

Essien fired in a speculative shot but two wicked deflections off Nemanja Vidic and Ferdinand saw the ball run into the path of Lampard, who slotted home a neat finish, dedicating the goal to his late mother Pat, who had died in April.

This surprise equaliser transformed Chelsea and during the next quarter of an hour they ran the show, passing the ball around with purpose and running freely behind United defenders.

The much-criticised Luzhniki Stadium pitch in Moscow suddenly started to exert an influence and both Ferdinand and Lampard were treated for cramp.

Blues striker Drogba, who had been a peripheral figure for much of the game, suddenly produced a moment of brilliance with 13 minutes left, curling a shot against Van der Sar's post from 25 yards.

Then, with just 3 minutes remaining of normal time, there came a moment of history when Alex Ferguson brought on substitute Ryan Giggs in place of Scholes. This was the Welshman's 759th senior appearance for United, taking him past the previous club record held at the time by United legend Sir Bobby Charlton, who was watching from the stand.

Chelsea boss Avram Grant sent on his first substitute 2 minutes into extra time – Salomon Kalou taking over from Florent Malouda – and almost at once United were saved by the woodwork for a second time in the game. German star Michael Ballack brilliantly set up Lampard, whose shot rebounded to safety off Van der Sar's crossbar. That was close, mighty close!

United hit back and were left cursing their luck 10 minutes into extra time when Chelsea skipper John Terry rose superbly to head Giggs' effort off his own goal line after Patrice Evra had surged his way down the left.

Rooney, who had not been at his best, looked totally fed up when he was taken off and Nani brought on in the 101st minute. The Portuguese international certainly added more pace to the attack but United weren't playing well.

With 4 minutes remaining, Chelsea were reduced to ten men when Drogba was sent off for slapping Vidic after a 'handbags and gladrags' melee inside the penalty-area. At least eighteen players were involved, all arguing about the manner in which the ball should be put out of play after several had 'dropped' to the ground with cramp.

As the arguments continued, Terry tried to sort it out, but foolishly Drogba intervened as well and decided to have a swipe at Vidic. He was shown a straight red, while his colleague Ballack was booked for dissent.

This sparked United into life, but there was no breakthrough and the final went to penalties for the ninth time.

And this is how the dramatic shoot out transpired, with United going first:

Tevez (Manchester United) scored – 1-0
Ballack (Chelsea) scored – 1-1
Carrick (Manchester United) scored – 2-1
Belletti (Chelsea) scored – 2-2
Ronaldo (Manchester United) missed – 2-2
Lampard (Chelsea) scored – 2-3
Hargreaves (Manchester United) scored – 3-3
Ashley Cole (Chelsea) scored – 3-4
Nani (Manchester United) scored – 4-4
John Terry (Chelsea) missed – 4-4

Into sudden death:

Anderson (Manchester United) scored – 5-4
Kalou (Chelsea) scored – 5-5
Giggs (Manchester United) scored – 6-5
Anelka (Chelsea) missed – 6-5

Chelsea had the chance of winning at 4-4, but Terry slipped on his run up and fired against a post, allowing United off the hook and give them a massive lift.

Substitutes Anderson and Kalou traded successful kicks before the cool-headed Ryan Giggs threw all the responsibility on Nicolas Anelka's shoulders as the shoot-out reached sudden death. It proved all too much for the French striker, whose kick was palmed away by Van der Sar. United were duly crowned 'Kings of Europe' once again. Great stuff.

NB: During a training session two days before this game, United players had practiced taking penalties and Ryan Giggs was pleased he did!
    He said,

When I knew the game would go into a shoot-out, I thought I would aim for the corner. I felt that if I kept the same technique which I had used in training, and hit the ball low and hard towards the corner, it meant that if the keeper did save it, it would have to be a good save. It was a relief to see it go in, and of course it meant that Chelsea had to score the next one. As it was, Edwin saved Anelka's penalty and we had won. Great, absolutely great.

42

Manchester United 0 Arsenal 0
Premier League
16 May 2009

Everyone associated with Manchester United knew that a single point was required from their penultimate game of the season to clinch a third successive Premier League title.

United had already amassed eighty-six points; second-placed Liverpool, with a better goal-difference, were on eighty. It was close, but United were on a roll, having won seven League games on the bounce, including a 2-0 derby victory over rivals City and a resounding 5-2 win over Tottenham Hotspur.

Manager Alex Ferguson had virtually a full-strength squad to choose from, electing to start with Carlos Tevez up front ... his brilliant equaliser at Wigan in the previous game earning him a place ahead of Dimitar Berbatov.

Arsenal were lying fourth in the table, and had suffered a 4-1 home defeat at the hands of Chelsea six days earlier. Earlier in the season they beat United 2-1 at The Emirates and they knew that revenge would be the name of the game as far as United were concerned at Old Trafford!

Manchester United (4-4-2): Van der Sar; O'Shea, Vidic, Evans, Evra, Ronaldo, Fletcher, Carrick, Giggs, Rooney (Anderson), Tevez (Park).
Arsenal (3-1-4-2): Fabianski; Sagna, Toure, Gibbs (Eboue), Song, Nasri (Bendtner), Denilson, Diaby, Fabregas, Arshavin (Walcott), van Persie.
Attendance: 75,468

In front of a near full-house – just 301 below capacity – United clinched a third successive Premier League title (and their eleventh overall) by gaining the point they needed to equal Liverpool's long-standing record of eighteen top-flight championship victories. But let's be truthful, as Old Trafford's chief reporter Phil McNulty wrote: 'It was an afternoon gripped with tension', as battling Arsenal made them fight every inch of the way.

In fact, both Robin van Persie and Cesc Fabregas wasted good chances in the second half and victory for the Gunners would of course take the title race into a final week, and as a result leave United a bit of work do against Hull City.

As it was, United's defence held firm to deliver another clean sheet – their twenty-third of the League – and this was crucial, because up front their strikers never really got going due to some strong tackling by the Arsenal defenders.

Rooney missed United's best chance with a first-half header and out-of-sorts Carlos Tevez was substituted with 23 minutes remaining. In fact, Rooney and Cristiano Ronaldo were surprisingly kept under shackles for most of the game.

United were certainly not at their best, but all credit to Darren Fletcher and Nemanja Vidic who were outstanding.

Russian star Andrey Arshavin, restored to Arsenal's side after illness, had plenty of possession in a first half, and from his 13th minute cross Van Persie headed wide.

Rooney should have done better with a header from John O'Shea's cross 4 minutes later, yet with Arsenal seemingly getting a foothold in the game, United's defence never really looked under pressure. Nevertheless it was nail-biting stuff every time the Gunners crossed the halfway line.

United had an opportunity to go ahead just before the interval, but Ryan Giggs, who would soon be collecting his eleventh Premier League winner's medal, shot well over the top after some smart work by Rooney.

Van Persie, already on a yellow card for a reckless challenge on Ronaldo, was fortunate to escape with a lecture from referee Mike Dean early in the second period for another bad tackle, this time on Patrice Evra.

United, struggling to create a clear-cut opening, brought a blocked save from Fabianski just past the hour mark but Ronaldo blasted the loose ball well over the bar.

That was Tevez's last contribution, although the home fans didn't appreciate Ferguson's decision to replace him with Park. In fact, the substitution was met with some derision.

As he left the pitch, Tevez waved to all sides of the ground in an apparent farewell, although he would make his final appearance for the club in the Champions League final.

Ronaldo thought he had scored with 12 minutes remaining, but his 20-yard free-kick dipped just wide with Fabianski well beaten.

Then, with Arsenal looking relaxed, Fabregas almost stunned Old Trafford with 7 minutes left. Left in space, a yard or so inside the penalty area, he could only find the side-netting, to the relief of the home fans.

Moments later, Van Persie shot straight at Van der Sar as United closed ranks, but there was still enough time left for the Dutch striker to give the home faithful one final scare, smashing in a free kick which was thankfully blocked by Michael Carrick.

Seconds later, referee Dean sounded the final whistle and United were crowned champions again.

Nothing, however, could overshadow United's achievement. The joy of players, the fans and the management was overwhelming as the presentations were made after the final whistle with club captain Gary Neville lifting the coveted Premier League trophy.

Arsenal manager Arsene Wenger said after the game, 'United are worthy champions. They did well in every single competition and that is very difficult. It was a very interesting championship. I think United won it because they got more points at home than any of the other teams in the top four.'

Alex Ferguson responded, 'The great challenge now is to try to win it next year because that would be something special. A nineteenth League title would give us a special place in the club's history.'

Next up for United was the Champions League final against FC Barcelona, and victory over the Spanish club would see the Reds become the first team to defend the European title since the name of the competition was changed in 1992.

43

Manchester United 0 FC Barcelona 2
Champions League Final
27 May 2009

Having already played twelve games in the competition, and sixty-five in total during the season, United were confident they could retain the Champions League trophy at the expense of Barcelona, who had already completed the Spanish La Liga and Copa del Rey double.

Alex Ferguson had a big decision to make ... should he play Rio Ferdinand, who had appeared in only one of the last nine League games, or go with Jonny Evans or Phil Neville? Also, should he start with Nani, Dimitar Berbatov or Carlos Tevez or start with all three? In the end he went for experience as the team line-up shows.

As for Barcelona boss Pep Guardiola, he also had a few worries, and these were in defence, but he had sufficient cover and put out a very strong side, as always.

United had scored eighteen goals and conceded just six in their twelve Champions League games so far; Barcelona had netted thirty and given away thirteen. They had beaten Bayern Munich 4-0 in a quarter-final tie and knocked Chelsea out in the semi-finals. United meanwhile had taken care of Arsenal in the semis having earlier defeated Celtic, Inter Milan and Porto.

FC Barcelona (3-2-3-2): Valdes; Puyol, Pique, Sylvinho, Busquets, Toure, Iniesta (Pedrito), Xavi, Eto'o, Messi, Henry (Keita).
Manchester United (4-4-2): Van der Sar; O'Shea, Ferdinand, Vidic, Evra, Carrick, Park Ji-Sung (Berbatov), Anderson (Tevez), Giggs, Ronaldo, Rooney.
Attendance: 62,467

'Manchester United fold without a fight as Barcelona claim Champions League'... that was Kevin McCarra's headline to his report in the *Guardian* newspaper.

United trooped off the Olimpia Stadio pitch bruised and beaten and if the truth be known they were lucky to get away with a 2-0 defeat! Alex Ferguson's team was outclassed by rookie Pep Guardiola's side, who won in style.

United had coped with the Spanish giants the previous season, drawing 0-0 at the Camp Nou and winning 1-0 at Old Trafford, but this time round it looked like giants against men!

At times it was embarrassing for United as Barça's sublime midfield quartet of Yaya Toure, Iniesta and Xavi, plus the brilliant Lionel Messi, completely ran the show.

United's frustrated substitute Paul Scholes should have seen at least a red card for one of two reckless two-footed tackles in the last 15 minutes of the game, but referee Massimo Busacca let him off lightly by giving him a stern lecture!

This was, in fact, United's first defeat in a final of a major European tournament, but few could have envisaged Barcelona could produce such a terrific performance against the Premier League champions, especially with a makeshift back four. But in all honesty, Barça's defence was never under pressure!

Michael Carrick, Anderson and Park Si-Jung were bemused in centre-field, and the latter two were replaced by Carlos Tevez (on 46 minutes) and Dimitar Berbatov (66). Ryan Giggs tried his best, having a couple of decent runs, but he had no support, not even from the out-of-sorts Wayne Rooney or Cristiano Ronaldo!

Messi and co. simply ran rings around most of the United players, and the little Argentinian celebrated by scoring his side's second goal, leaping to head home a deep cross from Xavi in the 70th minute. This, by the way, was Messi's first goal against an English team in a Champions League fixture after ten previous blanks.

Former Arsenal star Thierry Henry should have scored for Barça in the second half. Xavi also hit a post with a free kick and both Messi and Samuel Eto'o, also went close.

Despite the absence of Eric Abidal, Daniel Alves and Rafael Marquez at the back Barcelona were always in control of the game, although an early free kick by Ronaldo was blocked tentatively by goalkeeper Victor Valdes before the ball was thumped behind for a corner.

On 10 minutes, Iniesta conned Anderson and Carrick before picking out Eto'o who bamboozled Nemanja Vidic before angling his shot past Edwin van der Sar at his near post to give Barça the lead.

United never recovered, but some say they gave up far too easily. But one mustn't forget, you have to get the ball first before mounting an attack. And Barça rarely gave it away!

Before half-time Messi, Henry (twice) and Busquets all tested Van der Sar and during the first period of the second half Messi (again) and Toure came close to adding a second goal for the Spanish club.

Soon after Messi had bagged his goal, Ronaldo had a half-chance in a scramble inside the 6-yard box but the ball was cleared and with it went any hope of a United revival.

It was hard-going chasing the ball, and the exhausted look on the faces of the United players was evident well before the close.

Afterwards, a bitterly disappointed Giggs said, 'We were second best, no question about that. Their passing was inch-perfect and we were given a good old beating by a class team.'

It was hard to realise at the time that United had already won the Premier League title, the League Cup and the FIFA World Club Cup. They were quietly confident of course of lifting the Champions League trophy, but in Rome they met opponents who produced celestial football. 'Well played Barcelona – you were terrific,' said Alex Ferguson.

Manchester United 3 Bayern Munich 2
(4-4 aggregate, United lost on away goal rule)
Champions League, Semi-Final 2nd Leg
6 April 2010

Wayne Rooney had been nursing an ankle ligament injury, sustained in the first game in the Allianz Arena eight days earlier, and was doubtful for the return leg, while Ryan Giggs, who had started only one Premier League game since mid-February, was certainly not 100 per cent fit. In the end the England striker was selected by Alex Ferguson, but Giggs started on the bench along with Dimitar Berbatov.

United were still on course for the treble – the League Cup (already won), the Premier League title (still battling it out with Chelsea) and of course the Champions League. The games were coming thick and fast, so too were injuries. Nevertheless, Ferguson had a strong squad and in an interview before the second leg against Bayern Munich, he said, 'We're up for this ... let the show begin.'

Ryan Giggs added, 'It will be tough, we all know that, but we have the players, the skill and the experience to win the tie.'

As for Bayern, they were on course to win their twenty-second Bundesliga title and they were also waiting to play Werder Bremen in the German Cup final, which they would win by 4-1 to complete a domestic double.

For the record, a crowd of 65,931 had attended the first leg in Germany which Bayern won 2-1 with goals by Ribery (76 minutes) and Olic (90), with Rooney on target as early as the 2nd minute for United. Giggs came on as an 82nd minute substitute.

Manchester United (4-4-2): Van der Sar; Rafael, Ferdinand, Vidic, Evra, Valencia, Fletcher, Carrick (Berbatov), Gibson (Giggs), Nani, Rooney (O'Shea).
Bayern Munich (4-4-1-1): Butt; Van Buyten, Demichelis, Lahm, Badstuber, Ribery, Van Bommell, Muller (Gomez), Schweinsteiger, Robben (Hamit Altintop), Olic (Pranjic).
Attendance: 74,482

On a night of passion, commitment, nervous tension and excitement, Arjen Robben's spectacular goal ended Manchester United's hopes of reaching a third successive Champions League final.

The former Chelsea star smashed home a magnificent volley from Franck Ribery's corner kick with just over a quarter of an hour remaining of this tightly fought quarter final second leg encounter at Old Trafford. This brought the aggregate scores level at 4-4 but Bayern Munich went through on the away goal rule, following United's 2-1 defeat in Germany.

It looked as though United would cruise into the semi-finals after going 3-0 up before the interval, giving them an overall lead of 4-2. But things were to change dramatically as the game progressed.

Rooney was into the action straightaway and, as Bayern's defence backed off, he set up Darron Gibson, whose right footed shot flew past Hans-Jorg Butt to put United in front after just 3 minutes.

4 minutes later it was 2-0. Antonio Valencia tormented Holger Badstuber and crossed for Nani to flick the ball beyond Butt and into the far corner.

Bayern simply couldn't contain United at this point. Their defence was in tatters and a wild clearance from Butt almost let in Carrick, but he shot wide.

Rooney then came out a tackle limping heavily. It was several minutes before he was able to run freely, much to the relief of the United bench.

Bayern were well and truly on the rack. They were being run ragged by a purposeful United, and Rafael was guilty of wasting a great opportunity to increase United's advantage on 34 minutes when he charged into the box, only to fire across the face of goal instead of passing to the unmarked Rooney for a tap in.

After Van der Sar had saved at the feet of Ivica Olic, it came as no surprise when Nani scored his second, and the Reds' third, goal as half-time approached.

Valencia was again the provider. His high cross went over Rooney's head, but dropped at the feet of the Portuguese international who netted with a power drive high past Butt.

The whole mood and shape of the tie, however, was turned on its head a minute before the break when Olic, taking advantage of poor defending by Carrick, managed to bundle the ball over the line to bring the Germans back into contention.

Managed at the time by future United boss Louis van Gaal, Bayern came out with all guns blazing at the start of the second half, and after United's Rafael had been dismissed after picking up a second yellow card for hauling back Ribery, Ferguson immediately took off the limping Rooney and brought on John O'Shea.

The momentum, however, had swung Bayern's way and they began to run the show, creating space and opening up United's defence at will. Ribery had a volley punched away by Van der Sar before United counter-attacked with Patrice Evra, whose astute pass found Nani in space, but his effort was blocked by Butt.

Darren Fletcher also managed to get in a shot but generally it was all Bayern.

After their substitute Mario Gomez had flicked Philip Lahm's cross against the crossbar, with Van der Sar beaten, United conceded a second goal on 74 minutes – a wonder strike from Robben which stunned Old Trafford!

The wide man was left unmarked at the far corner of the area and his superb low left-footed volley flew into the net like a rocket with Van der Sar having no chance whatsoever of saving.

Giggs came on for Gibson with 9 minutes remaining and he certainly livened up proceedings, but time was running out fast. Ferguson also introduced Berbatov as he waved his players forward in search of another goal, but it was all too late, and although Giggs and Nani tried their best, the Bayern back-line held firm. United had nothing left and they slipped out of the competition, beaten effectively by Robben's 'away' goal.

Ferguson's men had certainly suffered a severe body-blow by losing to Bayern, and now the boss had to get his team back together for one final assault at winning a fourth successive Premier League title. United had six games remaining; they won five and drew one, but it wasn't enough and they were pipped at the post by Chelsea, 86 points to 85.

N.B. Bayern reached the final but lost 2-0 to Inter Milan in Madrid.

45

Manchester United 1 FC Barcelona 3
Champions League Final
28 May 2011

This was Manchester United's fourth Champions League final and their sixth major European showdown in forty-three years – taking in their 1968 European Cup and 1991 Cup Winner's Cup victories. And they knew, long before kick-off, they would have to be 'on top of their game and produce an outstanding performance' to beat Barcelona at the new Wembley Stadium

Defeated 2-0 in the 2009 final by the Spanish club, United wanted revenge big time, but manager Alex Ferguson, chewing away at his gum, said 'It's going to be tough, mighty tough.'

En route to the final, United had conceded only four goals in twelve games, beating, among others, Rangers and Valencia in Group C, Olympique Marseille in the knockout stage, Chelsea over two legs in the quarter-final and FC Schalke 6-1 on aggregate in the semis.

Barcelona had also played twelve games, winning eight and drawing three, scoring twenty-seven goals and conceding eight. Among their victims were Arsenal and La Liga rivals Real Madrid, who they defeated in the semi-finals, winning 2-0 in the Bernabeu and drawing 1-1 at home. Their biggest win had been 5-1 over Shakhtar Donetsk in a quarter-final leg.

Barcelona had already won the La Liga title but had lost to Real Madrid in the Copa del Rey final. They desperately wanted to add the Champions League prize to their collection, so too did United, who had clinched the 2011 Premier League crown earlier in the month. Let the game begin!

FC Barcelona (4-4-1-1): Valdes; Dani Alves (Puyol), Pique, Mascherano, Abidal, Busquets, Iniesta, Xavi, Pedro (Affelay), Messi, Villa (Keita).
Manchester United (4-4-2): Van der Sar; Fabio (Nani), Ferdinand, Vidic, Evra, Carrick (Scholes), Park, Valencia, Giggs, Hernandez, Rooney.
Attendance: 87,695

Football correspondent Duncan White wrote in the *Telegraph*:

> Beneath the soaring Wembley arch, Barcelona ascended to new heights. Inspired by an exhilarating Lionel Messi, Pep Guardiola's team swept past Manchester United in a thrilling performance and, with their third Champions League title in the last six seasons, they earned the right to be called one of the very greatest club sides in the history of the game.

Hear, hear.

United did threaten occasionally through Wayne Rooney, and he scored a terrific equaliser 11 minutes before the interval, but ultimately Barcelona were far too good for Alex Ferguson's men.

Realistically speaking, although it was 1-1 at half-time the Spaniards should have been at least three goals ahead!

They made up for those missed chances in the second half, however, with goals from Lionel Messi and David Villa as United were given a lesson on how to play possession football and strike hard when required.

The game, over the whole 90 minutes, was especially good for the neutral and perhaps more so for the Barcelona supporters and the match statistics don't lie!

Barça had nineteen attempts on goal to United's four; they had two-thirds of possession, completed 667 passes to United's 301 and at times were in total control.

All credit to the United boss who was gracious in defeat and quick to congratulate Barcelona. 'They were far better than us; we were well below par and the best team won by a mile,' said Fergie.

Not wanting a repeat of United's 2009 defeat Ferguson, along with his coaching staff, he spent a fortnight on the training pitch trying to conjure up a way of disrupting Barça's intricate passing game. He thought he had conquered it – until the match started!

He chose a team containing two strikers and two wingers, and after 10 minutes had passed, the plan was working.

Indeed, United began well, showing commitment and aggression, with Park Ji-sung making three superb tackles in the opening 5 minutes alone, including one real cruncher on Messi.

Barcelona's defence, without the leadership of Carles Puyol, looked rattled and Victor Valdes had to race off his line to punch the ball away from Rooney, while for United Gerard Pique almost conceded an own goal when pressurized by Javier Hernandez.

However, once United's initial thrust had passed, Barcelona took over with Xavi and Messi the key figures.

Villa fired wide and soon afterwards had another effort saved by Edwin Van der Sar. Two timely tackles on Messi by first Nemanja Vidic and then Rio Ferdinand averted danger but it was plain to see that United were being pushed back.

They were struggling to keep the ball and when they did get hold of it and pumped it forward, Hernandez, looking nervous, was repeatedly caught offside.

It came as no surprise when Barça took the lead on 27 minutes. Andres Iniesta exchanged passes with Sergio Busquets before spearing the ball through to Xavi. Ryan Giggs was not close enough to the midfielder who drove on towards the penalty area. Head up, he clipped a superb pass with the outside of his boot to Pedro, who evaded Patrice Evra, and before Vidic could get across, the ball was in the back of Van der Sar's net. Incredibly, this was Barcelona's 150th goal of the season.

With Ferguson animated on the touchline, frustrated at the way his team were surrendering possession, he suddenly leaped with joy when Rooney grabbed an equaliser.

Collecting a loose ball on the right, Rooney played a smart one-two with Michael Carrick before surging towards the danger-zone. He flicked the ball to Giggs who looked offside, but the Welshman cushioned it with his thigh and fed it back to Rooney whose powerful shot flew past a startled Valdes.

Barcelona responded with brilliant free-kick routine involving Xavi and Busquets which almost set up Pedro and then Messi, after a mesmerising run which took him past Vidic and Carrick, picked out Villa whose return cross was just ahead of the Argentina forward.

United simply couldn't get out of their own half as Barcelona held onto the ball.

9 minutes into the second half, United fell behind for a second time. Iniesta and Xavi worked the ball to Messi, who drove towards the edge of the penalty area before firing in a low into the net. He should have been closed down but was simply too quick for anyone to get near him.

United's keeper saved from Messi with his legs before denying Xavi as Barça went in search of more goals. And it was no surprise when a third arrived on 70 minutes.

Messi once again went hard at United's defence and when the ball broke to Busquets, he rolled it to Villa. His control was excellent and his dipping shot, into the top corner, sheer perfection.

United tried to get back into the game and Rooney found the roof of the net from outside the box and Giggs was convinced he was fouled inside the penalty, but Hungarian referee Viktor Kassai waved play on. This action showed the mental strength of Rooney and Giggs, who refused to give up despite Barça's undoubted superiority.

46

Manchester United 8 Arsenal 2
Premier League
28 August 2011

United had started the season well, beating neighbours Manchester City 3-2 in the FA Community Shield and West Bromwich Albion 2-1 away and Tottenham Hotspur 3-0 at home in the Premier League.

Arsenal had yet to score in 2011/12, drawing 0-0 at Newcastle and losing 2-0 at home to Liverpool, both in the Premier League. And manager Arsene Wenger had already used fewer than nineteen players in those opening two matches.

Reigning champions United, in fact, had won eight and drawn two of their last eleven Premier League games, their only defeat coming against Arsenal at The Emirates, when they went down 1-0 on May Day.

Ryan Giggs had so far played once as a substitute (v. Spurs) and once again he started on the bench as manager Alex Ferguson chose to go with Ashley Young (out wide), Tom Cleverley, Nani and Anderson across midfield against the Gunners.

Manchester United (4-4-2): De Gea; Smalling, Jones, Evans, Evra, Anderson (Giggs), Nani (Park Ji-Sung), Cleverley, Young, Rooney, Welbeck (Hernandez).
Arsenal (4-4-1-1): Szczesny; Jenkinson, Koscielny, Djourou, Traore, Rosicky, Ramsey, Arshavin, Coquelin (Oxlade-Chamberlain), Walcott (Lansbury), Van Persie (Chamakh).
Attendance: 75,448

On the very same day that United went goal-crazy against a depleted Arsenal side, the other team in Manchester – City – whipped Tottenham Hotspur 5-1 at White Hart Lane to make it a 13-goal bonanza against London opposition.

This game at Old Trafford had virtually everything – a missed penalty, a converted spot-kick, a hat-trick for Wayne Rooney, a red card, six yellows and of course plenty of goals. United were stupendous, romping to a resounding 8-2 victory and Ryan Giggs only played the last quarter of the game. What might the score have been had he started?

Ashley Young (2), Nani, Danny Welbeck and substitute Park Ji-Sung also found the back of the Gunners' net, while United's goalkeeper David De Gea brilliantly saved a penalty when the lead was a slender one. Theo Walcott and Robin van Persie replied for the crestfallen visitors, who had right-back Carl Jenkinson red-carded in the second half.

United made their intentions clear from the first whistle as Welbeck raced in on Arsenal's keeper Wojciech Szczesny. The first two efforts came from Tom Cleverley and Welbeck as United's passing was swift and direct. Rooney and Nani followed up with two more shots on target as Ashley Young began to cause problems down the left.

It was no surprise when United took the lead on 22 minutes. Anderson lofted the ball over a spread-eagled Arsenal defence for Welbeck to steer home a looping header.

Chris Smalling then pulled his shot wide after creating space but then, against the run of play, referee Howard Webb awarded Arsenal a penalty for a tug by Jonny Evans on Walcott's shoulder. Thankfully, De Gea dived to his right to turn van Persie's spot-kick round the post.

The corner came to nothing and in United's next attack on 28 minutes, Arsenal found themselves two down. The lively Young seized on a weak header from Armand Traore and, taking careful aim, curled an inch-perfect shot past Szczesny.

De Gea was in action again soon afterwards, making a double save from Andriy Arshavin and van Persie, but United were on fire and Welbeck almost made it three with a diving header from Rooney's cross. Unfortunately, a hamstring injury ruined the young striker's afternoon (he was replaced by the Mexican Javier Hernandez on 35 minutes) while at the other end of the pitch, Arshavin, who had already been booked, flashed a shot over the bar.

United came again ... Cleverley was denied by Szczesny, Nani failed to convert a Young cross when a goal looked a certainty and Anderson shot wide before Arsenal's defence conceded again in the 41st minute. Jenkinson, who was lucky not to receive a red card for hauling down Young, stood in the wall as Rooney powered the free-kick past him and Szczesny to give United a 3-0 lead.

Rooney, who earlier had attempted to beat Szczesny from inside his own half, was now United's all-time record scorer in the Premier League.

However, with seconds remaining in the first half, complacency at the back allowed Arsenal into the game, Tomas Rosicky setting up Walcott whose drive from a tight angle whistled through De Gea's legs for 3-1.

In the dressing room, manager Ferguson stressed to his players that the game was still far from over, and, taking the hint, United shot out of the blocks with venom at the start of the second half. Szczesny saved from Young and Nani's chip was off target but the Gunners responded and De Gea was forced into a diving save from Van Persie's volley while Arshavin fired a yard or so wide after a slip by Smalling.

United's former Fulham defender then raced forward and, ignoring the overlapping Phil Jones, fed Rooney instead. He slipped in Nani who went through to score with an outrageous finish: 4-1 with 26 minutes remaining.

Nani and Anderson were then replaced by Ryan Giggs and Park Ji-Sung but the relentless attacking continued and almost immediately Giggs came close to scoring.

And after 'Man of the Match Rooney' had clipped a shot against an upright, Nani exchanged passes with Young to drill a low shot into the corner of the net for United's fifth goal in the 67th minute.

Goal number six followed 3 minutes later – Park lashing home an unstoppable drive after the Arsenal defence had been sliced open.

In the 74th minute, and completely out of the blue, van Persie restored a semblance of pride with an exquisite finish after being played onside by Jones but United simply stepped up a gear again.

Jenkinson received a second yellow card for barging over Javier Hernandez as he darted towards goal. Rooney stepped up to seal his hat-trick with an 82nd minute penalty: 7-2. And it got even worse for the Londoners when Young curled the ball home from a Giggs pass for United's eighth with a barely minute remaining.

Park shot over in stoppage time before the home fans celebrated after seeing their heroes inflict upon Arsenal their biggest-ever Premier League defeat and their heaviest in League football, in terms of goal difference, since 1927 when they lost 7-0 to West Ham. The Gunners' heaviest League defeat of all-time is 8-0 against Loughborough Town in 1896.

Although he was on the field for a relatively short time, Giggs created one of United's goals, and therefore this epic win is included as one of his 'Fifty Defining Matches'.

47

Manchester United 4 Chelsea 5
(after extra time)
League Cup, Round 4
31 October 2012

Amazingly, Alex Ferguson made ten changes from the team that had beaten Chelsea 3-2 at Stamford Bridge in a controversial and sometimes ill-tempered Premier League game just three days earlier, when Chelsea striker Fernando Torres was sent off. The only player who kept his place was full-back Rafael Da Silva.

As for Chelsea, John Mikel Obi and Juan Mata, the players who were at the centre of the initial allegations against referee Mark Clattenburg in the previous encounter, were both named in manager Roberto Di Matteo's line-up.

At the time, United were second in the League table, having won six of their opening eight games. Chelsea were top with seven wins to their credit.

And in the third round of the League Cup, United had knocked out Newcastle 2-1 while Chelsea had defeated Wolverhampton Wanderers 6-0.

Chelsea (4-4-1-1): Čech; Azpilicueta, Cahill, Luiz, Bertrand, Romeu (Oscar), Mikel (Ramires), Moses, Mata, Piazon (Hazard), Sturridge.
Manchester United (4-4-2): Lindegaard; Da Silva, Wootton, Keane, Büttner (Powell), Anderson (Tunnicliffe), Giggs, Fletcher, Nani, Hernandez, Welbeck (Macheda).
Attendance: 41,126

After that narrow win on Chelsea soil, this re-match – played on a miserable, wet Halloween night in South-west London – developed into a real humdinger of a cup tie.

There were more moments of controversy, as usual, but the overall play by both teams was something special, although perhaps not in the eyes of the respective managers!

United had the better of the first half and led 2-1 at half-time with goals from Ryan Giggs and Javier Hernandez while David Luiz struck home a penalty for Chelsea.

Gary Cahill pulled Chelsea level again early in the second half before Portuguese international Nani made it 3-2 to United just before the hour mark. This goal seemed to have booked United a place in the quarter-finals, only for Chelsea to storm back once more and grab a life-saving third equaliser courtesy of Eden Hazard's late, late penalty.

This took the tie into extra time and this time it was the home side who went in front, Daniel Sturridge netting on 97 minutes to make it 4-3. That changed to 5-3 with 4 minutes remaining, Ramires virtually sealing victory with the cutest of finishes. But back came United and, with referee Lee Mason having already looked at his watch, Giggs stepped up to score his second goal of the evening from the 12-yard spot.

But the repercussions of United's narrow 3-2 win at the weekend were impossible to ignore and a group of United fans unfurled a banner which read 'Clattenburg. Referee, Leader, Legend' and there were also loud chants aimed towards Chelsea defender John Terry, who was in the stand serving the third game of his four-match ban for racially abusing Anton Ferdinand.

The Brazilian midfielder Anderson and substitute Nick Powell had excellent games for United, as did thirty-eight-year-old Ryan Giggs who – surprisingly – was on the field for the entire 120 minutes. Victor Moses was Chelsea's most influential player ahead of Ramires and Oscar, who ran the show when they were introduced in the second half.

With Torres suspended, Daniel Sturridge made his first start of the season for Chelsea and he had the game's first shot on goal. But after that the twenty-three-year-old Sturridge was well marshalled by United's young central defensive pairing of Scott Wootton and Michael Keane.

United took the lead in bizarre circumstances in the 22nd minute. After a free-kick from full-back Alex Büttner floated wide, Petr Čech restarted play by sending his goal-kick to Oriol Romeu, who was dispossessed by Anderson who quickly passed to Giggs who scored as Luiz ambled back on to the pitch.

Chelsea hit back strongly, and after half an hour Büttner fouled Moses inside the penalty area, allowing Luiz to gleefully convert from the spot.

United's second goal came in the 43rd minute. An attempted shot by Luiz cannoned back into his own half where Hernandez, showing good pace, exploited the huge gap to go on and score his fourth goal in three games.

With United's young defence looking in control, Chelsea suddenly broke out and drew level 7 minutes after the restart, Gary Cahill powering home a header from Juan Mata's corner.

Then it was action at the other end of the field as Nani, who had not been seen at all, suddenly burst into life to net United's third goal. He played a quick one-two with Anderson, burst into space and finished with his right foot. The only thing Petr Čech could do in the Chelsea goal was to collect a bottle which had been hurled on to the pitch.

Di Matteo urged his players to get forward and after, Cesar Azpilicueta had been closed down at the far post, Chelsea's claims for a penalty were dismissed when Mata's shot hit Keane's hand.

In the 4th minute of stoppage time, however, referee Mason did point to the spot after Wootton clumsily fouled Ramires. The cool-headed Hazard converted down the middle and at last Chelsea were cock-o-hoop and United under pressure.

7 minutes into extra time, Sturridge pounced on a poor headed back-pass by Wootton, rounded Anders Lindegaard and put Chelsea in front.

Keane was fortunate to receive only a yellow card for dragging back Sturridge before Ramires danced through United's defence to put the match beyond doubt with 4 minutes remaining. But United still had something, left and right at the death Giggs converted a penalty after Azpilicueta had fouled Hernandez. In the end, however, time ran out for the Reds as the Blues gained sweet revenge. As one newspaper heading stated, it was 'Capital punishment for Reds reserves.'

In the next round Chelsea beat Leeds 5-1 but were then knocked out by Swansea City in the semi-finals.

48

West Bromwich Albion 5 Manchester United 5
Premier League
19 May 2013

This was to be Sir Alex Ferguson's 1,500th and last game in charge of Manchester United. His first was back in November 1986 when United lost 2-0 away against Oxford United in a Division One encounter.

Regarded as the greatest football club manager of all-time (certainly by United fans) he had already guided the Reds to a record-breaking thirteenth Premier League title (finishing ahead of arch-rivals Manchester City) and he certainly wanted to go out on a high with a win over eighth-placed West Bromwich Albion, who they had beaten 2-0 at Old Trafford earlier in the season. He made several changes from the side that had defeated Swansea City in their last home game of the campaign, choosing to leave Rio Ferdinand, Ryan Giggs and Paul Scholes (ready for his last appearance for the club) all on the bench. And there was no Wayne Rooney, goalkeeper David De Gea, Nemanja Vidic or Patrice Evra.

The hosts Albion had lost five of their previous seven League games, including a 4-0 drubbing at Norwich City a week earlier, and they had yet to beat United in the Premier League, but manager Steve Clarke was adamant that his team 'had been playing well and would give United a run for their money.'

West Bromwich Albion (4-4-1): Foster; McAuley, Olsson, Ridgewell (Lukaku), Dorrans, Yacob, Morrison (Fortune), Mulumbu, Brunt, Long (Rosenberg).
Manchester United (4-4-2): Lindegaard; Valencia, Jones, Evans (Ferdinand), Büttner, Anderson, Carrick, Cleverley (Giggs), Kagawa (Scholes), van Persie, Hernandez.
Attendance: 26,438

Although he was only a substitute, coming on with half an hour remaining, Ryan Giggs had a fine game at The Hawthorns – United's defence didn't!

This was the first 5-5 draw in Premier League history (1992–2013) and if both teams had taken other chances which came their way, the final scoreline might well have been 7-7, even 8-8!

For the neutral it was a cracking game of football. However, for both sets of supporters, it was somewhat tense and as for the managers, well, they were scratching their heads from the first to the last whistle!

On the day of his farewell party, Sir Alex Ferguson requested that his players express themselves in his final game in charge and they certainly did that in an attacking sense during an unbelievable encounter.

The Scot saw his side throw away 3-0 and 5-2 leads as history was made at The Hawthorns – this being the first 5-5 draw ever in the Premier League, while at the same time it was United's first such scoreline since November 1895 when they shared ten goals with Lincoln City in a Second Division game, while for the Baggies it was their first five-all encounter in a major competition.

In an end-to-end thriller, Shinji Kagawa, Alex Büttner, Robin van Persie, Javier Hernandez, and an own goal by Swedish defender Jonas Olsson, scored for United, and substitute Romelu Lukaku, with a hat-trick, and James Morris and Youssef Mulumbu netted for Albion whose battling performance earned them a deserved point while at the same time ensured Sir Alex's career ended on a slightly disappointing note. But I don't think anyone cared really … it was a day and a game to remember.

The atmosphere inside the ground was electric as United, having already clinched the Premier League title, along with the boss, Sir Alex, came out to a guard of honour. With both sets of players and the crowd applauding, the stage was set for an occasion befitting the great man's last ever stint in the dugout.

With 3,000 United fans packed into the Smethwick End of the ground, the action from the start was simply sensational … and it was United who struck the first blow as early as the 6th minute. Büttner's pass into the right-hand channel looked to be going out of play but Hernandez chased it down, looked up and crossed superbly for Kagawa to head down and past former United goalkeeper Ben Foster.

3 minutes later Kagawa, avoiding a stumble by van Persie, found wing-back Antonio Valencia out wide. He wasted no time in driving the ball across goal, where the unfortunate Olsson deflected it past Foster to double United's lead. This was the third goal given away by an Albion defender in the last four games.

The Reds were on fire, and as van Persie chipped for goal, the ball flicked out off Olsson and out for a corner.

Phil Jones saw a shot loop up for Foster to catch and Hernandez, whose attacking play was terrific, missed the target with a free header from captain Michael Carrick's cross.

On the half-hour mark, United went three up. Carrick's pass was dummied by both Hernandez and Tom Cleverley, allowing Büttner to smash the ball hard and low into the far corner of the net. The goal triggered dissent from the home fans but it seemed to spark the Baggies into life and Shane Long headed over.

Soon afterwards, Hernandez should have netted a fourth for United but his shot lacked accuracy. And in Albion's next attack, they scored when Morrison beat Jones to steer Graham Dorrans' low cross past Anders Lindegaard for 3-1.

Both sides came close again before half-time. Valencia and Cleverley set up Hernandez whose shot was straight at Foster. The ball cannoned goalwards off McAuley but the Baggies' keeper reacted by making a stunning tip-over save. And then a slip by Jones let in Morrison, but Jonny Evans was there to make an excellent saving challenge as Long looked certain to fire home.

Baggies' boss Steve Clarke introduced Chelsea loanee Lukaku at the start of the second half and straightaway the Belgium international charged into the heart of the United defence.

Indeed, within 5 minutes the Belgium international found the net when his weak shot was pushed into the net by Lindegaard, who knew he should have done better.

United were now under pressure but they responded in emphatic style with Valencia again to the fore. In the 53rd minute, he once again darted down the right before whipping over a wonderful low cross which was driven high into the net by van Persie. It was the Dutchman's thirtieth goal of his debut campaign for the Reds.

After McAuley had stopped Hernandez in his tracks, and Valencia had made an important clearance at the other end, Giggs came on to join the cavalry. And almost immediately he zipped down the left wing, collected Kagawa's pass and delivered a perfect cross for Hernandez to tap in his fiftieth goal for the club on 63 minutes.

Albion should have reduced the deficit when Olsson skied the ball over from a couple of yards out while Lukaku hammered a free-kick wide and the skimmed the side-netting from another promising position. The warning signs were there; United were again on the back foot.

Büttner hit the bar and Giggs chipped onto the top of the net, as United attempted regain the initiative, but it was the Baggies who were in control. And in an amazing yet crazy finale, they scored three times to earn a creditable draw.

On 80 minutes, after Dorrans and Billy Jones had both come close, Lukaku ran onto Markus Rosenberg's through ball to net his second goal (3-5) and within a minute, from their very next attack, Youssef Mulumbu strode through, unchallenged, to touch home Jones' pass to pull Albion back to within goal. Roared on by their fans, the Baggies went for broke and with time running out Paul Scholes picked up a booking on his final appearance for United, while Rio Ferdinand was introduced in a bid to stem the tide. However, the veteran centre-back was unable to clear when Lukaku threatened again and the striker was strong enough to bundle the ball over the line from virtually a horizontal position to sensationally level at 5-5 and stun United, Fergie and indeed Giggs!

It was not the parting result Sir Alex wanted, or deserved, but all credit to Albion who made this into one hell of a football match. As he waved farewell to the United supporters, Fergie reflected that any more matches like this would not be good for his blood pressure!

After the game, Giggs – who still had one more season in him as a United player – said, 'This was one of the best games I have seen and played in. It was a great advert for Premier League and, indeed for British football.'

N.B. After twenty-seven years in charge, Ferguson bowed out as United's manager with this impressive record: Matches: 1,500, won 895, drawn 338, lost 267.

49

Manchester United 4 Norwich City 0
Premier League
26 April 2014

Former Preston North End boss David Moyes left Everton to officially take over from Sir Alex Ferguson as United's manager on 1 July 2013. However, on 22 April 2014, with the Reds in seventh position in the Premier League and having just been beaten 2-0 by his former club, Everton, as well as being out of all three major Cup competitions, he was sacked after barely ten months at the helm.

Soon after Moyes' departure, United's vice-chairman Ed Woodward named Ryan Giggs as the club's interim manager for the remaining four games of the season ... at home to Norwich City, Sunderland and Hull City and away to Southampton.

At his first press conference as 'manager' Giggs told the reporters: 'I'm nervous as hell. But everyone's behind me and I've had so many complimentary and good luck messages from the supporters. I'm looking forward to my first game in charge – let's hope we can claim a victory.'

For the visit of the Canaries to Old Trafford, Giggs made six changes to the team that had wilted at Goodison Park, and he said, 'I want my players to show passion, speed, tempo, bravery and imagination'.

Norwich, deep in trouble and languishing in seventeenth position in the table, had lost eight of their previous twelve League games, and they had caretaker/manager Neil Adams in charge. He had taken over from Chris Hughton just three weeks earlier.

In the game at Carrow Road in late December, a second-half goal by Danny Welbeck had given United a 1-0 victory.

Manchester United (4-4-2): De Gea; Jones, Ferdinand, Vidic, Evra, Valencia, Carrick, Cleverley (Hernandez), Kagawa (Young), Welbeck, Rooney.
Norwich City (4-5-1): Ruddy; Whittaker, Turner, Martin, Olsson, Johnson, Snodgrass, Fer (Tettley), Howson, Redmond (Hooper), van Wolfswinkel (Elamander).
Attendance: 75,208

It all went according to plan, as they say. United played well, albeit against moderate opposition, as Ryan Giggs made a winning start to his brief managerial reign at Old Trafford.

Wayne Rooney and substitute Juan Mata both scored twice to see off Norwich and so keep the Reds in contention for a place in the Europa League for 2014/15.

Rooney opened the scoring with a 41st minute penalty and added a second with a curling effort early in the second half. Spanish midfielder Mata netted a third on 57 minutes and rounded things off with a smart 6-yard header with 18 minutes remaining.

A rapturous welcome greeted Giggs as he emerged from the tunnel, with a record 962 appearances for the club already behind him. A 'good luck' card from the club's mascot 'Fred the Red' was also presented to him.

There was nothing worthwhile to write home about after a rather tepid opening 30 minutes, although Norwich goalkeeper John Ruddy had to save smartly from Welbeck and also Antonio Valencia.

Norwich, facing a fifth successive defeat, sat back but there was no way they were going to spoil the day for Mr Giggs.

With half-time approaching Rooney took centre stage by stroking home a penalty to give United a deserved lead, sending Ruddy the wrong way from the spot after Steven Whittaker was adjudged by referee Lee Probert to have fouled Welbeck.

Then, 3 minutes after the resumption, the England striker scored his nineteenth goal of the season – firing the ball home, in off the post from 25 yards, despite losing his footing.

Welbeck – one of six changes made by Giggs from that debacle at Everton – saw a well-drilled smart half volley saved by Ruddy before he was replaced by United's record signing Mata on the hour mark.

Ruddy then denied Rooney hat-trick before Mata, with his third touch, volleyed in Phil Jones's cross from six yards to give United a 3-0 lead.

The Spaniard looked a different class as he teased the Norwich defence with some clever passes, and it was only right that he should score again, heading in Valencia's cross-shot for his fifth United goal with more than a quarter of an hour left to play.

During that time, Javier Hernandez should have scored a fifth for United but missed a one-on-one chance, while Norwich substitute Johan Elmander fired wide and Martin Olsson saw his effort deflected against the crossbar. But there was only going to be one winner on the day – Manchester United – as Giggs celebrated his first win as a club manager!

Norwich never recovered. They were relegated in eighteenth position.

50

Manchester United 3 Hull City 1
Premier League
6 May 2014

This game saw Ryan Giggs make his last appearance as a Manchester United player and, indeed, his last as a footballer in any competitive match.

This was, of course, only his third game in charge at Old Trafford, having won one and lost one of his previous two.

He named two teenagers in his starting line-up against the Tigers – Welsh U21 midfielder Tom Lawrence and England youth striker James Wilson – and he also brought back two Belgians, Marouane Fellaini and Adnan Januzaj, while naming himself on the subs bench along with Robin van Persie and Nemanja Vidic.

Hull City, managed by the former United defender Steve Bruce, were sitting nervously in fifteenth position in the Premier League table. In fact, the Tigers had won only two of their previous eleven games and had lost 3-2 at home to United earlier in the season.

Manchester United (4-4-1-1): De Gea; Valencia, Smalling, Jones (Vidic), Büttner, Carrick, Kagawa, Januzaj, Wilson (van Persie), Fellaini, Lawrence (Giggs).
Hull City (4-1-4-1): Jakupovic; Elmohamady (Livermore), Davies, A. Bruce, Rosenior (Sagbo), Figueroa, Meyler, Quinn, Long (Fryatt), Koren, Boyd.
Attendance: 75,341

This wasn't a stroll in the park for United. They had to work hard for their victory against a resilient Hull City side who certainly gave a good account of themselves in an enthralling contest.

In the end United just about deserved their win and duly completed a Premier League double over the gritty Tigers.

Eighteen-year-old Wilson scored twice on his debut to help Giggs' new-look United to their nineteenth win of the season but only their ninth at Old Trafford.

The Reds had looked comfortable during the first half hour, yet created few chances. Then, perhaps surprisingly, Wilson notched the first of his brace after 31 minutes. Fellaini headed down a free-kick for the teenager to smash the ball into the net between the legs of exposed goalkeeper Eldin Jakupovic from 8 yards – an unforgettable start to his United career.

The impressive Wilson went close to adding another goal to his tally early in the second half, but saw his effort fly over the bar after good work from his co-debutant Lawrence. A couple of attacking substitutions by Hull boss Bruce opened the game out more in the second half and it was the lively Januzaj who went close to scoring with a rasping drive which Jakupovic pushed wide.

United doubled the lead just after the hour when Wilson pounced on a rebound from Fellaini's shot, but Hull hit back immediately and Matty Fryatt curled a beauty round David De Gea from long range – a superb goal.

Giggs then replaced Wilson with van Persie and soon afterwards the interim boss came on himself at the expense of Lawrence. And right away the Welshman was rolling back the years with a couple of incisive runs that clearly disturbed the Hull defence.

But Hull were still in the game, giving their all, and David Meyler's fierce 30-yard drive produced a fine save from De Gea. Then van Persie curved a shot a yard or so wide before the Dutchman made sure of all three points with an excellent strike from the edge of the box, after some excellent work by Giggs. With time running out, Jakupovic denied the 'boss' a goal with a flying save from his free kick.

After this win, Giggs had one game left in charge – away at Southampton. This ended all square and afterwards he admitted to breaking down in tears, in part due to the pressure of managing Manchester United. And he also admitted that he had struggled to get to sleep during his time as manager.

The game at Southampton was, in fact, United's 5,390th in competitive football.

When Dutchman Louis van Gaal was appointed as Moyes' permanent replacement on 19 May 2014, he named Giggs as his assistant manager, while at the same time the Welshman, now forty years of age, was praised for giving debuts to youngsters James Wilson and Tom Lawrence in the victory over Hull.

For the record, United came seventh in the Premier League in 2013/14 – their lowest placing for almost a quarter of a century, since finishing thirteenth in 1989/90. But it was no fault of Ryan Giggs!

Also Available from Amberley Publishing

Fifty matches that defined the career of one of the world's most famous footballers.

Paperback
168 pages
978-1-4456-4641-1

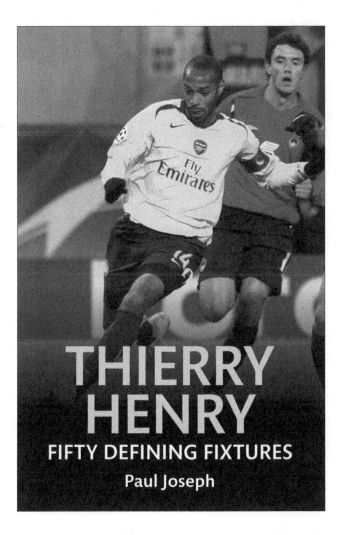

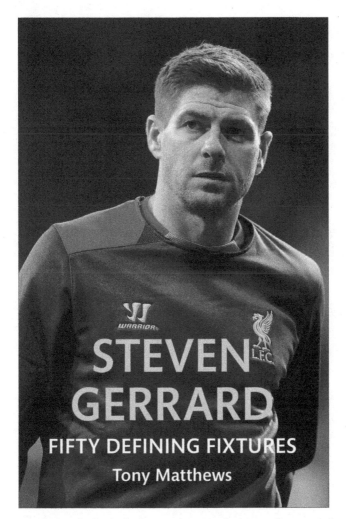

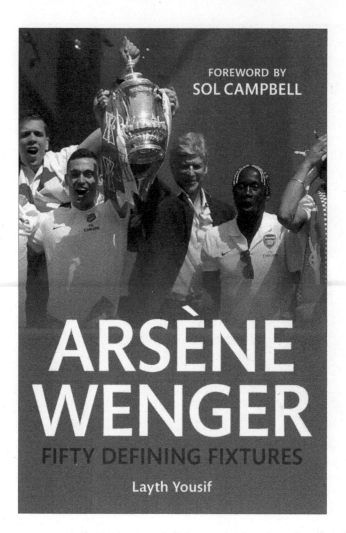